KILLING GIANTS, PULLING THORNS

CHARLES R. SWINDOLL

MULTNOMAH PRESS

Other Multnomah Press books by Charles Swindoll:
For Those Who Hurt
Second Wind: A Fresh Run at Life

PHOTOGRAPHY CREDITS: Russ Lamb; pages 6, 19, 20, 30, 75, 82 and cover.
Dewit Jones; pages 5, 11, 38, 43, 53, 54, 70 and 95
DESIGN BY: Dannelle Pfeiffer

FIRST PRINTING, 1978

Printed in the United States of America
Library of Congress Catalog Card Number: 78-57675
ISBN: 0-930014-22-7

GIANTS

Big things.
Things that buffet, bluster
 . . . and defy domination.
Dark things.
Ominous shadows that blight, blacken
 . . . and blot out the Son.

"Now then, give me the hill country
that the Lord promised me . . .
The giants are there in large walled cities . . .
The Lord will be with me and
I will drive them out . . . ."

—Caleb

THORNS

Little things.
Things that prick, penetrate
    . . . and progressively poison.
Unexpected things.
Low-lying vines that trip, tangle
    . . . and eventually imprison.

"The thorns which I have reaped
are of the tree
I planted; they have torn me,
and I bleed.
I should have known what fruit
would spring from such a seed."

                    —Byron

FOREWORD

In experiencing *Killing Giants, Pulling Thorns*, by Charles R. Swindoll, I have been transported into a world of vision, language and encouragement rarely encountered in my reading. Not since being captivated by *The Pilgrim's Progress* have verbal pictures so spoken to my need and filled me with insight and hope.

As every reader of Christian devotional literature knows, suffering cannot be explained away . . . nor can fear, bitterness, lust, jealousy, and other "giants" that stand against the work of the Holy Spirit in us. But the painful reminders of our humanity can be surrounded by a framework for understanding and resources for growth and faithfulness. Charles Swindoll's *Killing Giants, Pulling Thorns* helps to fill that need for me and many of my friends.

On a day alone, and between planes in the Denver airport, a friend slipped up to me while I was talking on the telephone. He introduced me without speaking to Dr. Swindoll's ministry of comfort. I was struggling with a personal issue and *For Those Who Hurt* met me in my insufficiency. It became clear to me as I paged through that gift book that truly affliction is for the comfort and salvation of others.

The exciting language and captivating photos of *Killing Giants, Pulling Thorns* combine to further ease the struggle and renew the heart. Dr. Swindoll's startling stories, precise phrases, honest judgments and Biblical teachings cause me again and again to sigh with recognition and nod with approval. This book will be a classic to return to on numerous occasions in our various moods and cares.

Mark O. Hatfield
United States Senate

KILLING GIANTS, PULLING THORNS

GIANTS

KILLING GIANTS

Giants are tough.

It's easy to talk about how you'd handle them as long as they are miles away, lumbering across someone else's landscape. But it's something else when you find yourself nose to knee with one on your **own** doorstep.

I know. I've faced several in my front yard—on my campus—in my church—on the silent battleground of my own soul.

People like us need the kind of faith young David showed when he plunged his hand into the cold stream, grabbed a fistful of stones and strode off to keep an appointment with the original Bigfoot—a fella named Goliath.

So let's face these giants together, okay? The intimidating Goliaths on the hill eclipse the Son only as they are standing and shouting—never after they're slain. They don't seem nearly so fierce in the prone position.

So let's kill 'em. One by one. With the sling of faith, the stone of truth and the name of the Lord of hosts as our battle cry.

THE SHADOW OF THE GIANT

Goliath reminds me of the cross-eyed discus thrower. He didn't set any records . . . but he sure kept the crowd awake!

Day after day, he paraded along the slopes of the Valley of Elah throwing out threats and belching blasphemies across the creek with a basso-profundo voice like 20 out-of-tune tubas. He was not only ugly, he was huge, well over 9 feet tall in his stocking feet. His armor included a bronze coat of mail weighing 200 pounds, a solid-iron spear (the head alone weighed 25 pounds), and a big bronze helmet. Add another club, bronze leggings and boots, plus that face of his . . . and you've got the makings of a shoo-in linebacker for the Chicago Bears, or next season's center for UCLA's starting five. Pity the poor private who drew duty as Goliath's shield bearer! It was about as suicidal as a novice drifting into the Devil's Triangle on a hang glider. Goliath, you see, was the pride of Philistia; and if you didn't believe it, all you had to do was ask him, or ask Saul's army (if you could find them).

Paralyzed and hypnotized, the camp of the Israelites sat galvanized in their tents. The only noise heard from the Israeli troops was the knocking of their knees or the chattering of their teeth—in unison. Goliath was, up to that point, emi- nently successful with his basic strategy of intimidation. His threats boomed across the valley with chilling regularity, producing the desired result: *fear*. The inspired record informs us that those monotonous blasts from the giant's mouth sounded forth every morning and every evening for 40 long days. The dawn of that 41st day, however, was the beginning of the end for the giant from Gath.

Some ten miles away a handsome, muscular teenager—the runt in a family of eight boys—was sent on an errand by his father. That innocent errand proved to be an epochal event in Jewish history. Fresh from the wilderness, the sheep trails and, more importantly, from the awesome presence of God, David stopped and stared in disbelief when he reached the battleground. For a young man whose unsullied character had been nursed in solitude and spawned in secret acts of bravery, the scene before him was staggering. The young shepherd simply could not believe his eyes. Refusing to accept his brothers' rationalizations or listen to the giant's threats, David saw through the Philistine strategy and withstood it through sheer, solid faith. You know the outcome. With a well-worn leather sling and a smooth stone, *and unbending confidence in his mighty God*, David introduced Goliath and all the Philistine hordes to the Lord of hosts, whose name they had blasphemed long enough. The account concludes with a profound statement:

> *Thus David prevailed over the Philistine with a sling and a stone, and he struck the Philistine and killed him; but there was no sword in David's hand (1 Samuel 17:50).*

What an interesting counterstrategy! To this day two timeless truths of giant warfare live on. Both are as appropriate today as they were in the days of Goliath.

Prevailing over giants isn't accomplished by using their technique. That's "lesson one" for all of us. Goliath might have been mistaken for the battleship *Missouri* with all his noise and iron and bronze. Not David . . . he didn't even carry a sword! His greatest piece of armor, the lethal weapon that made him unique and gave him victory, was his inner *shield of faith*. It kept him free from fear, it made him hard of hearing threats, it gave him cool composure amidst chaos, it cleared his vision.

Conquering giants isn't accomplished without great skill and discipline. To be God's warrior, to fight His way, demands much more expertise and control than one can imagine. Using the sling and stone of the Spirit is a far more delicate thing than swinging the club of the flesh. But oh, how sweet is the victory when the stone finds its mark . . . *and how final.*

Are you facing a giant? We're going to go through the files and pull the mug photos of 11 on the Lord's "Most Wanted" list. Chances are you've already bumped into one or more of them this week. Is the intimidation reaching unbearable proportions? Do your ears ache from their constant threats? Don't run . . . but don't try a bigger club, either. Be like David. Turn your Goliath over to Jehovah, the giant-killer. Explain to your powerful God how anxious you are for *Him* to win this victory for a change—not the giant, and not you.

Then load up your sling, soldier, and don't forget the stones. You're in for the time of your life.

FEAR

We were rapidly descending through a night of thick fog at 200 miles per hour, but the seasoned pilot of the twin-engine Aero Commander was loving every dip, roll and lurch. At one point he looked over at me, smiled and exclaimed, "Hey, Chuck, isn't this great?" I didn't answer. I was sweating it out on my knees.

As the lonely plane knifed through the overcast pre-dawn sky, I was reviewing every Bible verse I'd ever known and re-confessing every wrong I'd ever done. It was like hurtling 200 miles an hour down the Santa Ana Freeway with a white bedsheet wrapped across the windshield and your radio turned up just beneath the threshold of audible pain.

I couldn't believe my companion-in-flight. He was whistling and humming like it was all a bike ride through the park. His passenger, however, had ten finger-nails imbedded in the cushion. I stared longingly for something—*anything*—through the blanket of white surrounding us. Our flight record may have indi-cated two passengers on that eerie Monday morning, but I can vouch for at least three. An unyielding creature called Fear and I shared the same seat.

Fear—the phantom giant. Drifting in through cracks in the floorboards or filtering down like a chilling mist, the fog called Fear whispers omens of the unknown and the unseen. Surrounding individuals with its blinding, billowy robe, the creature hisses, "What if . . . what if . . .?" One blast of its awful breath transforms saints into atheists, reversing a person's entire mind-set. Its bite releases a paralyzing venom in its victim, and it isn't long before doubt begins to dull the vision. To one who falls prey to this attack, the creature displays no mercy. It falls full weight on his back, laughs with glee at its crippled plaything and circles for another savage assault.

Fear. Ever met this beast? Sure you have. It creeps into your cockpit by a dozen different doors. Fear of failure. Fear of heights. Fear of crowds. Fear of disease. Fear of rejection. Fear of unemployment. Fear of what others are saying about you. Fear of moving away. Fear of height or depth or distance or death. Fear of being yourself. Fear of buying. Fear of selling. Fear of financial reversal. Fear of war. Fear of the dark. Fear of being alone.

Lurking in the shadows around every imaginable corner, it threatens to poison your inner peace and outward poise. Bully that it is, the creature relies on scare tactics and surprise attacks. It watches for your vulnerable moment, then picks the lock that safeguards your security. Once inside, it strikes quickly to tranform spiritual muscle into mental mush. The prognosis for recovery is neither bright nor cheery.

David's 27th psalm, however, is known to contain an unusually effective antitoxin. With broad, bold strokes, the monarch of Israel (the first giant-killer on record), pens a prescription guaranteed to infuse iron into our bones. He meets Fear face-to-face at the door of his dwelling with two questions:

Whom shall I dread?
Whom shall I fear?

He slams the door in Fear's face with the declaration:

My heart will not fear . . . in spite of this I shall be confident (v. 3).

He then whistles and hums to himself as he walks back into the family room, kitchen, office or bedroom, reminding himself of the daily dosage required to counteract Fear's repeated attacks:

PRAYER: *I have asked from the Lord (v. 4).*
VISION: *I behold the beauty of the Lord (v. 4).*
GOD'S WORD: *I meditate in His temple (v. 4).*
GOD'S PROTECTION: *In the day of trouble He will conceal me/hide me/lift me*
                          (v. 5).
MOMENT-BY-MOMENT WORSHIP: *I will sing (v. 6).*
REST: *I had believed . . . wait for the Lord (vv. 13-14).*
DETERMINATION: *Let your heart take courage (v. 14).*

Oh, how I needed this prescription in that dark cockpit as we dropped thousands of feet through the fog. Could it be that a cold overcast obscures your horizons right now? Tell you what—let's share the same seat and relax for a change. God's never missed the runway through all the centuries of fearful fog.

But you might fasten your seat belt, friend. It could get a little rough before we land.

* * *

Too bad courage doesn't come in a neat foil packet like air-sick tablets. I have a friend who would have gladly bought out the drug store during a few dark days in Texas not long ago. Do you happen to remember that cantankerous lady named Miss Hurricane Carla? Let me tell you, she was a flirt.

She winked at Galveston, whistled at Palacios, waved at Corpus Christi, waltzed with Port Lavaca and walked away with Rockport, Arkansas Pass, and half of Matagorda Island. Her previous escort warned that she was a wicked woman, but few fishermen were ready to believe the rumors that blew in from the fickle waters of the gulf. Not only was she wicked, she was expensive and *mean*. That mid-September date ended up costing 400 million dollars . . . and 40 lives.

A friend of mine lived through that ordeal. He spent two terrible days and sleepless nights in his attic, surrounded by rattlesnakes, water moccasins and other sassy visitors who had been flushed out of their habitat. The screaming of Carla outside blended horribly with the bass rumblings of the giant named Fear. I would compare my friend's courage—and the courage of hundreds like him who endured Carla's rage—to anyone who has courted one of death's sisters and lived to describe the romance.

COURAGE. It has several names: bravery, valor, fearlessness, audacity, chivalry, heroism, nerve . . . and a few *nicknames:* guts, grit, gristle, backbone, pluck, spunk. But whatever the name, it's more than a match for Fear. The heights of the Himalayas only encourage it. The depths of the Caribbean merely excite it. The sounds of war stimulate it. The difficulty of a job motivates it. The demands of competition inspire it. Criticism challenges it . . . adventure arouses it . . . danger incites it . . . threats quicken it.

It's just another word for inner strength, presence of mind against odds, determination to hang in there, to venture, persevere and withstand hardship. It's got keeping power. It's what kept the pioneers rolling forward in those covered wagons in spite of the elements and mountains and flaming arrows. It's what makes the amputee reject pity and continue to take life by the throat. It's what forces every married couple having trouble *never* to say, "Let's terminate." It's what encourages the divorcee to face tomorrow. It's what upholds the young mother with kids in spite of a personal energy crisis. It's what keeps a nation free in spite of attacks. As Thomas Jefferson wrote in his letter to William Stevens Smith:

> *The tree of liberty must be refreshed from time to time with the blood of patriots and tyrants. It is its natural manure.*

COURAGE. It feeds on giants. David had it when he grabbed his sling in the Valley of Elah. Daniel demonstrated it when he refused to bow before Nebuchadnezzar's statue in Babylon. Elijah evidenced it when he faced the prophets of Baal on Carmel. Job showed it when he was covered with boils and surrounded by misunderstanding. Moses used it when he stood against Pharaoh in the court of Egypt, refusing to be intimidated. The fact is, *it's impossible to live victoriously for Christ without courage.* That's why God's thrice-spoken command to Joshua is as timeless as it is true:

> *Be strong and courageous (Joshua 1:6,7,9).*

Are you? Honestly now—are you? Or are you quick to quit . . . ready to run when the heat rises . . . when the shadow of the giant looms across your horizon?

Let it be remembered that real courage is not limited to the battlefield or the Indianapolis 500 or to tackling a prowler in your living room. The *real* tests of courage are much broader . . . much deeper . . . much quieter. They are the *inner* tests, like remaining faithful when nobody's looking . . . like enduring pain when the room is empty . . . like standing alone when you're misunderstood.

You may never be asked to share your attic with a rattler, land an airplane in blinding fog or battle with a high-pocketed Philistine. But every day, in some way, your courage will be tested. Your test may be as simple as saying "No," as uneventful as facing a pile of dirty laundry, or as unknown and unheralded as an inner struggle between right and wrong. God's medal-of-honor winners are made in secret because most of their courageous acts occur deep down inside . . . away from the acclaim of public opinion . . . up in the attic . . . alone with a giant.

BITTERNESS

During my hitch in the Marine Corps, my wife and I rented a studio apartment in San Francisco from a man crippled by a World War 2 injury. Captured at Wake Island and later confined for years in China, he was left partially paralyzed when an enemy soldier struck him with a rifle butt.

When I visited with this landlord, he'd tell one story after another of how barbarically he'd been treated. With vile language and intense emotion, he spoke of the tortures he'd endured and of his utter hatred for the Japanese. Here was a man who had been horribly wronged—without question. The constant misery and pain he lived with could not be measured. My heart went out to him.

But there was another factor which made his existence even *more* lamentable. Our landlord had become a bitter man. Even though (at that time) he was 13 years removed from the war . . . even though he had been safely released from the concentration camp and was now able to carry on physically . . . even though he and his wife owned a lovely dwelling and had a comfortable income, the crippled man was bound by the grip of *bitterness*. He was still fighting a battle that should have ended years before. In a very real sense, he was still in prison.

His bitterness manifested itself in intense prejudice, an acrid tongue and an everyone's out-to-get-me attitude. I am convinced that he was far more miserable by 1957 than he had been in 1944. There is no torment like the inner torment of an unforgiving spirit. It refuses to be soothed, it refuses to be healed, it refuses to forget.

In the New Testament, every mention of bitterness comes from the same Greek root, *pic*, which means "to cut, to prick." The idea is a pricking or puncturing which is pungent and penetrating. We read in Luke 22:62 that Peter "wept bitterly." He wept because he was pricked in his conscience. He was "cut to the quick," we would say. In Acts 8:23, a man was said to have been "in the gall of bitterness" when he wanted to appear godly and spiritually powerful. He was simply a religious phony, bitter to the core.

Hebrews 12:15 states that a root of bitterness can spring up and cause trouble, causing many to be defiled. You cannot nurture the bitterness plant and at the same time keep it concealed. The bitter root bears bitter fruit. You may think you can hide it . . . live with it . . . "grin and bear it," but you cannot. Slowly, inexorably, that sharp, cutting edge of unforgiveness will work its way to the surface. The poison seedling will find insidious ways to cut into others. Ironically, the one who suffers most is the one who lashes out at those around him. He becomes the victim of the giant he refused to slay.

How can I make such a statement? Because of the parable Jesus presented in Matthew 18. Find a Bible and read verses 21 through 35. The context is "forgiveness." The main character is a man who refused to forgive a friend, even though he himself had recently been released from an enormous debt he had incurred. Because of his tacit refusal to forgive, this bitter man was "handed over to the torturers . . . ." And then Jesus adds the punch line:

> *So shall my heavenly Father also do to you, if each of you does not forgive his brother from your heart (v. 35).*

Did you hear what He said? He said that we who refuse to forgive—we who live in the gall of bitterness—will become victims of torture, meaning intense *inner* torment. If we nurture feelings of bitterness we are little better than inmates of an internal concentration camp. We lock ourselves in a lonely isolation chamber, walled in by our own refusal to forgive.

Please remember—Jesus was speaking to His *disciples*, not unbelievers. A Christian is a candidate for confinement—and unspeakable suffering—until he or she fully and completely forgives others . . . even when others are in the wrong.

I can now understand why Paul listed bitterness *first* when he said:

> *Let all bitterness and wrath and anger and clamor and slander be put away from you, along with all malice. And be kind to one another, tender-hearted, forgiving each other, just as God in Christ also has forgiven you (Ephesians 4:31-32).*

For your sake, let me urge you to "put away all bitterness" *now*. Kill that giant with the smooth stone of forgiveness. There's no reason to stay in P.O.W. camp a minute longer. The escape route is clearly marked.

It leads to the cross . . . where the only One who had a right to be bitter wasn't.

JEALOUSY

Like an anger-blind, half-starved rat prowling in the foul-smelling sewers below street level, so is the person caged within the suffocating radius of selfish jealousy. Trapped by resentment and diseased by rage, he feeds on the filth of his own imagination.

"Jealousy," says Proverbs 6:34, "enrages a man."

The Hebrews used only one word for jealousy as the Old Testament was being written: *qua-nah*, which meant "to be intensely red." The term was descriptive of one whose face flushed as a sudden flow of blood announced the surge of emotion. To demonstrate the grim irony of language, "zeal" and "ardor" come from the same word as "jealousy."

Here is the way it works. I love something very much, indeed, *too much*. I pursue it with zeal. I desire, in fact, to possess it completely. But the thing I love slips out of my hands and passes into another's. I begin to experience the gnawing pangs of jealousy. Strangely, the feelings of zeal and love begin to change. By the dark, transforming power of sin, my love turns to hate. Once I was open, happy, filled to the brim with exquisite delight, but no longer! Now I am closed within a narrow compass of inner rage, intensely and insanely angry.

Jealousy and envy are often used interchangeably, but there is a difference. Envy begins with empty hands, mourning for what it *doesn't* have. Dante pictures it as a blind beggar whose eyelids are sewn shut. The envious man is unreasonable because he is sewn up within himself. Jealousy is not quite the same. It begins with full hands but is threatened by the loss of its plenty. It is the pain of losing what I have to someone else, in spite of all my efforts to keep it. Hence, the tortured cry of Othello when he fears that he is losing Desdemona:

> *I had rather be a toad*
> *And live upon the vapor of a dungeon,*
> *Than keep a corner in the thing I love*
> *For others' uses (Othello III.iii. 270).*

This was Cain's sin. He was jealous of Abel. He resented God's acceptance of his brother. No doubt, his face was red with emotion and his eyes filled with rage as God smiled on Abel's sacrifice. Not until Abel's warm blood poured over Cain's cruel hands did jealousy subside. Solomon might well have written the epitaph for Abel's tombstone:

> *Jealousy is as cruel as the grave,*
> *Its flashes are flashes of fire (Song of Solomon 8:6 RSV).*

Anyone who has experienced deliverance from this hellish giant knows only too well the savagery of its seizure. Jealousy will decimate a friendship, dissolve a romance, and destroy a marriage. It will shoot tension through the ranks of professionals. It will nullify unity on a team . . . it will ruin a church . . . it will separate preachers . . . it will foster competition in a choir, bringing bitterness and finger-pointing among talented instrumentalists and capable singers. With squint eyes the giant of jealousy will question motives and deplore another's success. It will become severe, suspicious, narrow and negative.

I know what I'm saying. I lived many of my earlier years in the dismal, gaseous subterranean pipelines of jealousy, breathing its fumes and obeying its commands. It was gross agony.

But finally, by the grace of Jesus Christ, I realized that I didn't have to live in darkness. I slew the giant and crawled out . . . and the releasing sunlight of freedom captured my heart. The air was so fresh and clean. Oh, the difference it has made! It is utter delight.

Ask my wife.

LUST

Samson was a he-man with a she-weakness. In spite of the fact that he was born of godly parents, set apart from his birth to be a Nazarite, and elevated to the enviable position of a judge in Israel, he never conquered a relentless giant named Lust. On the contrary, it conquered him. Several things that illustrate his lustful bent may be observed from the record of his life in the Book of Judges:

1. The first recorded words from his mouth were: *I saw a woman* (14:2).
2. He was attracted to the opposite sex strictly on the basis of outward appearance: *Get her for me, for she looks good to me* (14:3).
3. He judged Israel for 20 years, then went right back to his old habit of chasing women—a harlot in Gaza, and finally Delilah (15:20-16:4).
4. He became so preoccupied with his lustful desires, he didn't even know the Lord had departed from him (16:20).

The results of Samson's illicit affairs are familiar to all of us. The strong man of Dan was taken captive and became a slave in the enemy's camp, his eyes were gouged out of his head and he was appointed to be the grinder in a Philistine prison. Lust, the giant jailer, binds and blinds and grinds. The swarthy pride of Israel, who once held the highest office in the land, was now the baldheaded clown on Philistia, a pathetic hollow shell of humanity. His eyes would never wander again. His life, once filled with promise and dignity, was now a portrait of hopeless, helpless despair. Chalk up another victim for Lust. The perfumed memories of erotic pleasure in Timnah, Gaza and the infamous Valley of Sorek were now overwhelmed by the putrid stench of a Philistine dungeon.

Without realizing it, Solomon wrote another epitaph—this one for Samson's tombstone:

The wicked man is doomed by his own sins; they are ropes that catch and hold him. He shall die because he will not listen to the truth; he has let himself be led away into incredible folly (Proverbs 5:22-23 TLB).

The same words could well be chiseled in the marble over many other tombs. I think, for example, of the silver-throated orator of Rome, Mark Antony. In his early manhood, he was so consumed with lust that his tutor once shouted in disgust:

> *O Marcus! O colossal child . . . able to conquer the world but unable to resist a temptation!*

I think of the gentleman I met a few months ago—a fine itinerant Bible teacher. He said he had been keeping a confidential list of men who were once outstanding expositors of the Scripture, capable and respected men of God . . . who have shipwrecked their faith on the shoals of moral defilement. During the previous week, he said, he had entered the name of *number 42* in his book. This sad, sordid statistic, he claims, caused him to be extra cautious and discreet in his own life.

A chill ran down my spine when he told that story. No one is immune. You're not. I'm not. Lust is no respecter of persons. Whether by savage assault or subtle suggestion, the minds of a wide range of people are vulnerable to its attack. Sharp professional men and women, homemakers, students, carpenters, artists, musicians, pilots, bankers, senators, plumbers, promoters and preachers as well. Its alluring voice can infiltrate the most intelligent mind and cause its victim to believe its lies and respond to its appeal. And beware—this giant never gives up . . . it never runs out of ideas. Bolt your front door and it'll rattle at the bedroom window, crawl into the living room through the TV screen, or wink at you out of a magazine in the den.

How do you handle such an aggressive intruder? Try this: When Lust suggests a rendezvous, send Jesus Christ as your representative.

Have Him inform your unwanted suitor that you want nothing to do with him . . . *nothing*. Have your Lord remind him that since you and Christ have been united together, you are no longer a slave to giants. His death and resurrection freed you from sin's stranglehold and gave you a new Master. And before giving Lust a firm shove away from your life, have Christ inform him that the permanent peace and pleasure you are enjoying in your new home with Christ are so much greater than Lust's temporary excitement that you don't need him around any longer to keep you happy.

For sin's power over us was broken when we became Christians and were baptized to become a part of Jesus Christ; through his death the power of your sinful nature was shattered. Your old sin-loving nature was buried with him by baptism when he died, and when God the Father, with glorious power, brought him back to life again, you were given his wonderful new life to enjoy (Romans 6:3-4 TLB).

But Lust is persistent. If he's knocked on your door once, he'll knock again. And again. You are safe just as long as you draw upon your Saviour's strength. Try to handle it yourself and you'll lose—every time. This is why we are warned again and again in the New Testament to *flee* sexual temptations. Remember, Lust is committed to wage *war* against your soul—in a life-and-death struggle—in hand-to-hand combat. Don't stand before this mortal enemy and argue or fight in your own strength—run for cover. Cry out for reinforcement. Call in an air strike. If you get yourself into a situation that leaves you defenseless and weak, if your door is left even slightly ajar, you may be sure that the ancient giant will kick it open with six-guns blazing. So don't leave it open. Don't give Lust a foothold . . . or even a toehold.

Joseph was a dedicated, well-disciplined believer, but he was smart enough to realize he couldn't tease lust without being whipped. When it came time for a hasty exit, the son of Jacob preferred to leave his jacket behind rather than hesitate and leave his hide. But not Samson. Fool that he was, he thought he could cuddle lust, inhale its heady perfume and enjoy its warm embrace without the slightest chance of getting caught. What appeared to be a harmless, soft, attractive dove of secret love turned into a reeking nightmarish vulture.

Lust is one flame you dare not fan. You'll get burned if you do.

Samson would sign this warning in my place if he could, for he, being dead, yet speaks.

DEPRESSION

The smoky tones of Peggy Lee's voice occasionally blow across my mind like a sea breeze over a dry, sun-washed beach:

Is that all . . . is that all there is . . .?

With no bitterness intended, I ask that haunting question in the backwash of certain situations—and so do most of you. How much like the tide we are! When our spirits are high, we are flooded with optimism, hope and pleasant expectations. But when low, with our jagged barnacles of disappointment and discouragement exposed, we entertain feelings of raw disillusionment. We usually hide the plunging inner tideline from others, protecting ourselves with a thick coat of public image shined to a high-gloss finish with the wax of superficiality . . . embellished with a religious cliché or two. But all the while, at ebb tide within, cold winds blow across the empty, empty sand. And out of the deep crawls another giant—a dragon named Depression.

Now if you're the type who *honestly and truly* never gets low—never feels the oppressive pang of periodic depression (I'm sure there are few), then you'll not understand my paintings or choice of frames. But if you're like me, you'll need no guide to help you through this gallery where shadows cast their debilitating aura.

There are peculiar low tides that often follow a great victory.

Is that all . . . is that all there is to victory? Elijah asked that. Fresh off a stunning victory at Carmel, the prophet became vulnerable and frightened. Alone under the gnarled limbs of a twisted juniper tree, he cried out to God—not in spontaneous praise but overwhelmed with self-pity. Elijah suffered the low tide that often follows victory.

Then there are special low tides that accompany great vision.

Is that all . . . is that all there is to vision?

Paul asked that. Having taken gigantic strides into the vast regions of Asia and having forged out an impeccable theology that was to serve the church for

"While in the heights of accomplishing a vast, encompassing vision, Paul tripped and fell into a deep well of sudden despair."

centuries—the apostle was caught at low tide. He freely admits this in his second letter to friends at Corinth:

> We do not want you to be uninformed, brothers, about the hardships we suffered in the province of Asia. We were under great pressure, far beyond our ability to endure, so that we even despaired of life (2 Corinthians 1:8 NIV).

While in the heights of accomplishing a vast encompassing vision, Paul tripped and fell into a deep well of sudden despair. Weary, lonely and emotionally drained, the seasoned apostle hit bottom. Low tide occasionally accompanies vision, a malady not limited to century-one saints.

And there are those low tides that attach themselves to great valor.

Is that all . . . is that all there is to valor?

David asked that. He had killed a giant and married a princess. He was a fierce and resourceful front-line fighter but found himself the target of his own king's spear. Although a proven and dedicated warrior, unmatched in Israel's ranks for bravery, he was forced to flee. This sent him reeling, appearing insane before the king of Gath. The once-exalted man of valor now "scribbled on the doors of the gate and let his saliva run down into his beard" (1 Samuel 21:13). David had wrestled with bears, tackled sinewy lions, and leveled a 9-foot-9 Philistine . . . but he traded an external giant for an internal one and was now rendered helpless by a low tide. All his valor seemed only a cheap, empty dream.

Low tide . . . how painful *yet how essential*. Without it the changing ocean becomes a predictable, boring body of water with no mysterious marriage to the moon, lacking its romantic, magnetic appeal. Without it there would be no need for Elishas to minister to anguished Elijahs . . . no need for visionaries to fall in dependence on their faces before God . . . no need for the valiant to be reminded of their source of strength.

Is that all . . . is that all there is to low tides?

No, there is more, much more, most of which can never be described . . . only discovered.

LONELINESS

It is the most desolate word in all human language. It is capable of hurling the heaviest weights the heart can endure. It plays no favorites, ignores all rules of courtesy, knows neither border nor barrier, yields no mercy, refuses all bargains and holds the clock in utter contempt. It cannot be bribed; it will not be left behind. Crowds only make it worse, activity simply drives it deeper. Silent and destructive as a flooding river in the night, it leaves its slimy banks, seeps into our dwelling and rises to a crest of despair. Tears fall from our eyes as groans fall from our lips—but loneliness, that uninvited guest of the soul, arrives at dusk and stays for dinner.

You have not known the bottom rung of melancholia until loneliness pays you a lengthy visit. Peter Tchaikovsky knew. The composer wrote the following words in a minor key:

NONE BUT THE LONELY HEART CAN FEEL MY ANGUISH . . .

There is simply no other anguish like the consuming anguish of loneliness. Ask the inmate in prison this evening . . . or the uniformed man thousands of miles at sea or in some bar tonight . . . or the divorcee in that apartment . . . or the one who has just buried his or her life's companion . . . or the couple whose arms ache for the child recently taken . . . or even the single, career-minded person who prepares a meal for one and goes to bed early, *alone*, surrounded by the mute memory of yesterday's song and today's disappointment.

I've crossed paths with many who could echo Tchaikovsky's lament . . . like the little Norwegian widow in Boston who now lives alone with only pictures of him whom God took . . . like the young nurse in 1967 who, after a shattered romance and broken engagement, went back to the Midwest to start over . . . like the alcoholic who wept on my desk one wintry morning clutching the bitter note left by his wife and kids: "Goodbye, forever" . . . like the husband beside the fresh grave on a windswept hill, who sobbed on my shoulder, "What now?" . . . like the disillusioned teen-age girl, away from home and heavy with child—wondering, "How can I face tomorrow?"

Some time ago someone placed this ad in a Kansas newspaper:

I will listen to you talk for 30 minutes without a comment for $5.00.

Sounds like a hoax, doesn't it? But the person was serious. Did anybody call? You bet! It wasn't long before this individual was receiving 10 to 20 calls a day. The pang of loneliness was so sharp that some were willing to try *anything* for a half hour of companionship.

God knows, my friend, and He *does* care. Please believe that! He not only knows and cares—He understands, He is touched, He is moved. Entering into every pulse of anguish, He longs to sustain and deliver us.

In the strangling grip of Golgotha, our Saviour experienced the maximum impact of loneliness. For an undisclosed period of time, the Father forsook Him. His friends had already fled. One had betrayed Him. Now the Father turned away. In the bottomless agony of that moment, our Lord cried—He literally screamed aloud (Matthew 27:45-46). The loneliness of those dark moments as our Saviour carried our sin cannot be adequately pictured on paper. Cold print cannot convey it. But is it any wonder that He is now able to sympathize and enter in as we go to war against the giant called Loneliness? Those who bear the scars of battle need no explanation of the pain—only an invitation to share in the wound and, if possible, help in the healing.

When we are lonely, we need an understanding friend. *Jesus* is the One who "sticks closer than a brother." When we are lonely, we need strength to keep putting one foot in front of the other—*Jesus* is the One "who strengthens me." When we are lonely, we need to lift our eyes off ourselves. *Jesus*, the "Founder and Finisher" of the life of faith, invites us to fix our eyes on Him (Hebrews 12:1-3) and refuse to succumb.

Somehow, with a new focus, loneliness doesn't seem to set up camp in the soul like before. There really isn't room. Peace pitches the first tent.

Jesus answers Tchaikovsky with these words in a major key: NONE BUT THE TRUSTING HEART CAN KNOW MY DELIVERANCE!

RESENTMENT

Leonard Holt was a paragon of respectability. He was a middle-aged, hard-working lab technician who had worked at the same Pennsylvania paper mill for 19 years. Having been a Boy Scout leader, an affectionate father, a member of the local fire brigade, and a regular churchgoer, he was admired as a model in his community. Until . . .

. . . that image exploded in a well-planned hour of bloodshed one brisk October morning. Holt decided to mount a one-man revolt against the world he inwardly resented. A proficient marksman, he stuffed two pistols into his coat pockets—a .45 automatic and a Smith and Wesson .38—before he drove his station wagon to the mill. Parking quietly, he gripped a gun in each fist then slowly stalked into the shop. He started shooting with such calculated frenzy that it resembled a scene out of "Gunsmoke." He filled several of his fellow workmen with two and three bullets apiece, firing more than 30 shots in all . . . deliberately killing some of the men he had known for over 15 years. When a posse was formed to capture the man, they found him standing in his doorway, snarling defiantly:

"Come and get me, you ____; I'm not taking any more of your ____."

Total bewilderment swept over the neighborhood. Puzzled policemen and friends finally discovered a tenuous chain of logic behind his brief reign of terror. Down deep within the heart and soul of Leonard Holt rumbled the giant of resentment. The man who had appeared like a monk on the outside was seething with murderous hatred within. A subsequent investigation led officials to numerous discoveries yielding such evidence. Several of the victims had been promoted over him while he remained in the same position. More than one in his car pool had quit riding with him due to his reckless driving. A neighbor had been threatened then struck by Holt after an argument over a fallen tree. The man was *brimming* with resentful rage that could be held in check no longer.

Beneath his picture in *Time* magazine, the caption told the truth:
RESPONSIBLE, RESPECTABLE—AND RESENTFUL.

On the exterior, the man paraded a glaze of affection and respectability. While at church, he wore a smile that would make you think he held hands with Gabriel. He knew the hymns by heart. He spoke to his Scout troop with persuasive, gracious lips. For 19 years he did his work with commendable diligence, speaking daily words of kindness with his superiors. Then something snapped. His smile curled into a snarl. The veneer of tranquility erupted with volcanic force. The hymn-singing churchman became a profane infidel.

So it is with resentment. Allowed to fester through neglect, the toxic fumes of hatred foam to a boil within the steamroom of the soul. Pressure mounts to a maddening magnitude. By then it's only a matter of time. The damage is always tragic, often irreparable:

- a battered child
- a crime of passion
- ugly, caustic words
- loss of a job

- a runaway
- a bad record
- domestic disharmony
- a ruined testimony

None of this is new. Solomon described the problem long ago:

> *Pretty words may hide a wicked heart, just as a pretty glaze covers a common clay pot. A man with hate in his heart may sound pleasant enough, but don't believe him; for he is cursing you in his heart. Though he pretends to be so kind, his hatred will finally come to light for all to see (Proverbs 26:23-26 TLB).*

The answer to resentment isn't complicated, it's just painful. It requires *honesty*. You must first disclose and expose the giant. It then requires *humility*. You must confess it before the One who died for such sins. It may even be necessary for you to make it right with those you have offended out of resentful bitterness. Finally, it requires *vulnerability*—a willingness to keep that tendency submissive to God's regular reproof, and a genuinely teachable, unguarded attitude.

Nobody ever dreamed Leonard Holt lived with a giant named Resentment. And nobody dreams *you* do either.

Not yet. . . .

GRIEF

Two elementary-school boys were, for the first time in their lives, absolutely still. Deathly still. In separate pools of blood, each under a pale gray blanket, they awaited the arrival of the coroner. For them, school ended prematurely. With omnipotent authority, the grim reaper visited the vast metropolis of Los Angeles at the corner of Beach Boulevard and Rosecrans Avenue—unannounced and uninvited. In heavy traffic. In broad daylight. Death the Dictator came, saw, and conquered. He always does, which prompted George Bernard Shaw to write:

The statistics on death are quite impressive. One out of one people die.

But what about those who *live on*? Those who try to pick up the jagged pieces? As I stood there beside my oldest son, fighting back tears, trying to swallow that knot in my throat, I kept thinking about two families that would never be the same. Two mothers and dads, standing eye to eye with the giant of grief. I could paint a portrait of the coming days: indescribable sorrow, disillusionment, sleepless nights, endless reminders, paralyzing anxiety, that unendurable sense of loss, that numbing mixture of anger, helplessness, denial and confusion.

Let's pause here and pretend. Let's pretend you are the neighbor. One of those two grieving families lives next door. On an average Thursday afternoon, your phone rings . . . or a knock comes at the door. The information you hear stuns you. You're suddenly reeling, and you feel as if you're in a dream ("nightmare" might be a better word). Life screams to a halt. Thursday seems strangely sacred, almost eerie.

The grief of someone very near becomes so real you can taste it. The pain stabs deep and perhaps your first thought is, "Oh, how my heart goes out to _____!" Your second thought is, "What can I do to help? What would be the best expression of love, compassion and sympathy?"

Suddenly, you're stuck. There's no set of rules to follow—no handbook for

"So many grieving . . . so few comforting."

showing mercy. You hurriedly thumb through your Bible and find no sermon notes on "How to Sympathize." No, my friend, comfort for the sorrowing cannot be regulated and systematized. To go through programmed motions with the grieving turns you into a good candidate for another "Job's counselor" . . . and none of us wants that title. What *can* you do? What *should* you do . . . or not do? What could be said that might be appreciated and appropriate?

Be real. As you reach out, admit your honest feelings to your friends. If the news stunned you, say so. If you suddenly feel tears coming, cry. If you are overwhelmed with pity and compassion, admit it. You may be a Christian with a firm hope in a life hereafter, but you're also human. Don't hide that. It may be through that gate a path of friendship will develop.

Be quiet. Your presence, not your words, will be most appreciated. The thick mantle of grief has fallen upon your friend, bringing dark, unexplainable sorrow. An abundance of words and attempts to instruct will only reveal an insensitive spirit to the grieving. The Joe Baylys, in the course of several years, lost three of their children. In his book, *The View from a Hearse*, he shares his honest feelings when one of the children died:

> *I was sitting, torn by grief. Someone came and talked to me of God's dealings, of why it happened, of hope beyond the grave. He talked constantly. He said things I knew were true.*
>
> *I was unmoved, except to wish he'd go away. He finally did.*
>
> *Another came and sat beside me. He didn't talk. He didn't ask me leading questions. He just sat beside me for an hour and more, listened when I said something, answered briefly, prayed simply, left.*
>
> *I was moved. I was comforted. I hated to see him go.*

Be supportive. Those who comfort must have a tender heart of understanding. They don't come to quote verses or leave a stack of literature. They come simply to say they care. Nor do they attempt to erase today's hurt by emphasizing tomorrow's hope. They are committed to the support, the understanding of the grieving. Few things heal wounded spirits better than the balm of a supportive embrace.

A little girl lost a playmate in death and one day reported to her family that she

had gone to comfort the sorrowing mother. "What did you say?" asked her
father. "Nothing," she replied. "I just climbed up on her lap and cried with her."

That's being supportive.

Be available. Everybody comes around the first day or two. But what about a month later? After the flowers? Or five months later? After the grass grows over the grave? Life, like the muddy Mississippi, keeps rolling along. Unfortunately, so do the memories of that little fella whose place at the supper table remains vacant. If ever the comforting hand of a friend is needed, it is then—when *other* kids are going swimming and snitching cookies and riding bikes. Be committed to comforting later on as well as now. Your appropriate suggestions that will help them break the spell of grief (C.S. Lewis wrote of "the laziness of grief") will help them begin again.

Like Jesus with the sisters of Lazarus in the crucible of grief, be real (He wept), be quiet (He took their angry rebukes), be supportive (He was deeply moved), be available (He stayed by their side). No big sermons, no leaflets, no attempts to correct their misunderstandings, not even a frown that suggested disapproval. Killing this giant takes time! Our Lord believed, as we should, that we are healed of grief only when we express it to the full.

Perhaps this explains why so many are grieving and so few are comforting.

PAIN

They called him "Old Hickory" because of his tenacity and grit. His mother chose "Andrew" on March 15, 1767, when she gave birth to that independent-minded South Carolina rebel. Wild, quick-tempered, and disinterested in school, Andrew answered the call for soldiers to resist the British invasion at age 13. Shortly thereafter, he was taken prisoner. Refusing to black an enemy officer's boots, he was struck with a saber—Andrew's first introduction to an ugly giant known as Pain.

Although he bore the marks of the blow for the rest of his life, Andrew's fiery disposition never waned. A fighter to the core, he chose to settle arguments in duels and lived most of his days with two bullets painfully wedged in his body. After distinguishing himself on the battlefield, his name became a national synonym for valor and stern persistence. When politics nodded in his direction, "Old Hickory" accepted the challenge: first the Senate, then nomination for President. The shadow of Pain appeared again in another form as he lost a narrow race with John Quincy Adams.

Four years later, however, he ran again . . . and won! But pain accompanied the victory. Two months before he took office he lost his beloved wife, Rachel. Grief-stricken, the President-elect pressed on. Even as he was being sworn into office as our nation's seventh President, he fought the anguish of a raging fever caused by an abscess in the lung.

Some time later one of the bullets within him had to be surgically removed. He endured that operation—done without anesthetic—in typically courageous fashion. Even his political career was painful. A nasty scandal split his cabinet and critics clawed at him like hungry lions. Although he stood firm for many months, the telling signs of pain began to manifest themselves. He was one of the few men who left office, however, more popular than when he came. "For once, the rising was eclipsed by the setting sun," wrote a contemporary sage. And it was pain, more than any other single factor, which drew the qualities of greatness out of Andrew Jackson.

Pain humbles the proud. It softens the stubborn. It melts the hard. Silently and relentlessly, it wins battles deep within the lonely soul. The heart alone knows its own sorrow, and not another person can fully share in it. Pain operates alone; it needs no assistance. It communicates its own message whether to statesman or servant, preacher or prodigal, mother or child. By staying, it refuses to be ignored. By hurting, it reduces its victim to profound depths of anguish. And it is at that anguishing point that the sufferer either submits and learns, developing maturity and character; or resists and becomes embittered, swamped by self-pity, smothered by self-will.

I have tried and I cannot find, either in Scripture or history, a strong-willed individual whom God used greatly until He allowed them to be hurt deeply.

It was just such a person who wrote these words for all to read:

GUESTS

Pain knocked upon my door and said
That she had come to stay,
And though I would not welcome her
But bade her go away,

She entered in.
Like my own shade
She followed after me,
And from her stabbing, stinging sword
No moment was I free.

And then one day another knocked
Most gently at my door.
I cried, "No, Pain is living here,
There is not room for more."

And then I heard His tender voice,
"'Tis I, be not afraid."
And from the day He entered in,
The difference it made!

Martha Snell Nicholson

"Stealing your surge of motivation, he whispers the magic word—'Mañana . . .'"

PROCRASTINATION

Allow me to introduce a professional thief.

Chances are you'd never pick this slick little guy out of a crowd but many, over the years, have come to regard him as a formidable giant. Quick as a laser and silent as a moonbeam, he can pick any lock in your home or office. Once inside, his winsome ways will captivate your attentions. You'll treat him like your closest friend. Ah . . . but watch out. He'll strip you without a blink of remorse.

Master of clever logic that he is, the bandit will rearrange the facts just enough to gain your sympathies. When others call his character into question, you'll find yourself not only believing in him, but actually *quoting* and *defending* him. Too late, you'll see through his ruse and give him grudging credit as the shrewdest of all thieves. Some never come to such a realization at all. They stroll to their graves arm-in-arm with the very robber who has stolen away their lives.

His name? *Procrastination*. His specialty? Stealing time and incentive. Like the proverbial packrat, he makes off with priceless valuables, leaving cheap substitutes in their place: excuses, rationalizations, empty promises, embarrassment and guilt. Like most crooks, this pro hits you when you're weak—the moment you relax your defenses. You wake up on a Saturday morning. It's been a beast of a week. Insistent voices of neglected tasks echo in your head and plead for attention. Suddenly your con-artist appears and begins to bargain with you. By sundown he's gone . . . and so is your day . . . and so is your hope.

You step on the bathroom scales and blink in disbelief. The dial tells you the truth—but the thief offers another interpretation. Stealing your surge of motivation, he whispers the magic word—*mañana*—and you reach for a donut to celebrate your philosophy:

Never do today what you can put off till tomorrow.

You face a crucial decision this afternoon. It's been building up for two weeks. You've ignored it, dodged it, postponed it—but you must not do so any longer. Today is "D" day. You've talked yourself into it. Thirty minutes before the deadline, the thief offers the perfect alibi and back on the shelf goes your decision, growing another day larger.

No piper was better paid. No liar was more respected. No bandit better rewarded. No giant better treated.

You name it—he comes out a winner every time even though he's a hard-core outlaw. He can outtalk any student when it comes to homework. He can outthink any executive when it comes to correspondence. He can outwork any homemaker when it comes to vacuuming or doing dishes. He can outlast any parent when it comes to discipline. He can outsmart any salesman when it comes to selling. He has one basic product and he centers all his energy toward that single goal: defeat. By the sheer genius of suggestion he becomes the epitome of what he destroys: success.

There once lived a politician named Felix. He was a governor during the first century. Before him stood a prisoner named Paul. On two separate occasions, Felix listened to Paul tell his story, presenting in simple, clear terms the matter of faith in Jesus Christ. Felix heard every word but passed off the message with similar comments:

> *When Lysias the commander comes down, I will decide your case (Acts 24:22).*
>
> *Go away for the present, and when I find time, I will summon you (Acts 24:25).*

The governor heard Paul, but he listened to the thief. He intentionally put off the most significant moment of his life—a decision he will never forget. Never. Why? Because he listened to the wrong counsel. It was only a subtle suggestion. It wasn't a bold-face lie, like "There is no heaven," or, "There is no hell." It was simply, "There is no *hurry*." Thereby the grim thief won another victory of defeat.

"How can *I* win?" you ask. What's the secret—the formula—for escaping this thief's intimidating web? How can I stop the giant from breaking and entering?

It's really very simple . . . so simple you won't believe it. All it takes is one word, perhaps the easiest word to utter in our language. Properly used, that single syllable carries more weight than a ton of good intentions. The thief cannot endure the sound of it. It sends him fleeing in frustration. If you use it often enough, he might get tired of hearing it—and start leaving you alone.

Curious? I'll make you a deal. I'll tell you the word only if you'll promise to use it next time you're tempted to listen to the fast-talking time-embezzler. I have a warning, however. It may be easy to say—but it will require all the discipline you can muster to *mean*. To implement it will demand, in fact, the power of God Himself.

The word is "No."

RUMOR

Abraham Lincoln's coffin was pried open twice.

The first occasion was in 1887, 22 long years after his assassination. Why? You may be surprised to know it was *not* to determine if he had died of a bullet from John Wilkes Booth's derringer. Then why? Because a rumor was sweeping the country that his coffin was empty. A select group of witnesses observed that the rumor was totally false, then watched as the casket was resealed with lead.

A second time, 14 years later, the martyred man's withered body was viewed again—this time by even more witnesses. Why *again*? For the same grim purpose! Rumors of the same nature had again implanted doubts in the public's mind. The pressure mounted to such proportions, the same ghoulish, grotesque ceremony had to be carried out. In spite of the strong protests of Lincoln's son Robert, the body was exposed a second time. Officials felt the rumors should be permanently laid to rest along with the Civil War President. Finally—the corpse was securely embedded in a crypt at Springfield.

"How unfair!" you say. "Cruel," is a better word. But, you see, rumors are like that. Lacking authoritative facts and direct source, information is loosely disseminated, creating unrest and harm. It is pandered by the busybodies who cater to the sick appetite in petty people. Those who feed on rumors are small, suspicious souls. They find satisfaction trafficking in poorly lit alleys, dropping subtle bombs that explode in others' minds by lighting the fuse of suggestion. They find comfort in being only an "innocent" channel of the unsure information, *never* the source. The ubiquitous "they say" or "have you heard" or "I understand from others" provides a handy back door for the self-righteous peddlers of rumor.

"Have you heard that the Hysterical Concrete Memorial Church is about to split?"

"I hear Ferdinand and Flo are divorcing . . . they say she was unfaithful."

"I've heard his parents have a lot of money."

"Did you hear that Pastor Elphinstonsky was asked to leave his former church?"

"I was told their son is taking dope . . . got picked up for shoplifting."
"Someone said they *had* to get married."
"Somebody mentioned he is a heavy drinker."
"I heard she's a flirt . . . watch out for her."
"The word is out—he finally cheated his way to the top."
"It's a concern to several people that she can't be trusted."
In King Henry IV, Shakespeare observes:

> *Rumor is a pipe*
> *Blown by surmises, jealousies, conjectures,*
> *And of so easy and so plain a stop*
> *That the blunt monster with uncounted heads,*
> *The still-discordant wavering multitude,*
> *Can play upon it (II, induction, line 15).*

And how certain Christians can play that pipe! The sour melodies penetrate many a phone conversation . . . or mealtime discussion . . . or after-church "fellowship time" (what a name!) . . . or a leisurely evening with friends. Rumor is a monstrous giant, capable of prying open more caskets, exposing more closet skeletons and stirring up more choking, scandalous dust than any other tool on earth.

With this in view, I submit four suggestions for silencing rumor-mongers:

1. Identify sources *by name*. If someone is determined to share information that is damaging or hurtful, request that the source be specifically stated.

2. Support evidence *with facts*. Do not accept hearsay. Refuse to listen unless honest-to-goodness *truth* is being communicated. You can tell. Truth is rarely veiled or uncertain. Rumors fade when exposed to the light.

3. Ask the person, *"May I quote you?"* It's remarkable how quickly gossipers can turn four shades of red. Equally remarkable is the speed with which they can backpedal.

4. Openly admit, "I don't appreciate hearing that." This approach is for the strong. It might drive a wedge between you and the guilty, but it's a sure way to halt the regular garbage delivery to your ears.

* * *

On a windswept hill in an English country churchyard stands a drab, gray slate tombstone. Bleak and unpretentious, it leans slightly to one side, beaten slick and thin by the blast of time. The quaint stone bears an epitaph not easily seen unless you stoop over and look closely. The faint etchings read:

BENEATH THIS STONE, A LUMP OF CLAY,
LIES ARABELLA YOUNG,
WHO, ON THE TWENTY-FOURTH OF MAY,
BEGAN TO HOLD HER TONGUE.

The tongue. Rumor-mongers would be hard pressed to perform their avocation without it. But what a study in contrasts! To the physician it's merely a two-ounce slab of mucous membrane enclosing a complex array of muscles and nerves that enable our bodies to chew, taste and swallow. How helpful! Equally significant, it is the major organ of communication that enables us to articulate distinct sounds so we can understand each other. How essential!

Without the tongue no mother could sing her baby to sleep tonight. No ambassador could adequately represent our nation. No teacher could stretch the minds of students. No officer could lead his fighting men in battle. No attorney could defend the truth in court. No pastor could comfort troubled souls. No complicated, controversial issue could *ever* be discussed and solved. Our entire world would be reduced to unintelligible grunts and shrugs. Seldom do we pause to realize just how valuable this strange muscle in our mouths really is.

But the tongue is as volatile as it is vital. It was Washington Irving who first said, "A sharp tongue is the only edge tool that grows keener with constant use." It was James, the half brother of Jesus, who first warned:

The tongue is a fire . . . a restless evil and full of deadly poison . . . (James 3:6,8).

Verbal cyanide. A lethal, relentless, flaming missile which assaults with killing power, searing and destroying at will. A giant, indeed!

And yet it doesn't look anything like the brutal beast it is. Neatly hidden behind ivory palace gates, its movements are an intriguing study of coordination. It can curl itself either into a cheery whistle or manipulate a lazy, afternoon yawn. With no difficulty it can flick a husk of popcorn from between two jaw teeth or hold a thermometer just so. And it is *tricky*! It can help you enjoy the flavor of a stick of peppermint as it switches from side to side without once getting nipped. Moments later it can follow the directions of a trumpeter, allowing him to play "Flight of the Bumblebee" without a single miscue.

But watch out! Let your thumb get smashed with a hammer or your toe get clobbered on a chair and that slippery creature in your mouth will suddenly play the flip side of its nature.

Not only is the tongue untamed, it's *untamable*! Meaning what? Meaning as long as you live it will never gain control of itself. It defies being tamed. Incredible! We can tame Flipper and Trigger and Shamu and Lassie. We can train falcons to land on our wrists, pigeons to carry our messages, dogs to fetch the paper, elephants to stand on rolling balls, tigers to sit on stools and alligators to turn over and get their bellies rubbed. But the tongue? Impossible to train!

Many men before me have offered counsel on how to keep our tongues checked and caged. One was William Norris, the American journalist who specialized in simple rhymes that packed a wallop. He once wrote:

> *If your lips would keep from slips,*
> *Five things observe with care:*
> *To whom you speak; of whom you speak;*
> *And how, and when, and where.*

Publius, the Greek sage, put his finger on another technique we tend to forget when he admitted:

> *I have often regretted my speech, **never** my silence.*

King David put it even more bluntly in Psalm 39:

> *I will guard my ways,*
> *That I may not sin with my tongue;*
> *I will guard my mouth as with a muzzle (v. 1).*

That's what it takes. A tight, conscious muzzle on the muscle in your mouth. Harnessing such an elusive giant requires a determined mindset. With your Lord's help, take these three first steps:

Think first. Before your lips start moving, pause ten seconds and mentally preview your words. Are they accurate or exaggerated? Kind or cutting? Necessary or needless? Wholesome or vile? Grateful or complaining?

Talk less. Your chances of blowing it are directly proportional to the amount of time you spend with your mouth open. Try closing it for a while. Compulsive talkers find it difficult to keep friends. They're irritating. So conserve your verbal energy! Make your words like that nationally advertised shampoo: concentrated and richer.

Start today. Fit that muzzle on your mouth *now*. It's a project you've put off long enough. Arabella Young waited too long.

THORNS

PULLING THORNS

It is one thing to cross swords with those dark, hulking giants in life. But it's something else entirely to stumble into a briarpatch along the slopes. Sometimes a speck in the eye, a splinter in the finger or a rock in the shoe can be as bothersome as a giant on the hill.

Sometimes more.

So instead of whistling in the dark and pretending they're not there, let's get some light on those thorns that hinder our hope. It's time to cut back the thistles and clear out a place to stand . . . to walk . . . to run free.

THE STING OF THE THORN

Give the Reverend Dullard Drydust enough time and he will manage to confuse most sections of the Bible. Because we preachers are notorious for getting hung up on Greek tenses and purpose clauses and theological trivia, we often shy away from those passages that appear nontechnical and plain.

Like the parables, to be specific. Like Mark 4, to be exact. Not only is that particular parable simple and straightforward, it's even interpreted for us by Jesus, the One who thought up the story in the first place. And since it has to do with a farmer-type who pitches some seed on different kinds of soil, it doesn't seem to have the sophisticated ingredients needed for homiletical hash. After all, there's not a lot you can say about the story of a farmer who drops little seeds here and there in a haphazard fashion—*or is there*? At first glance, maybe not, but after some thought, I'm convinced there's more here than any of us ever dreamed. And since the Son of God explains its essential meaning, the story cannot be twisted nor forced to fit the fancy of some hungry-eyed pulpiteer looking for three points and a poem.

This is a profound story about life—real life—your life and mine. It boils life down to the four basic responses people have toward spiritual things. The "seed," according to the speaker, is the Word—God's Word, the truths of the Bible. The four different "soils" represent people of all ages and interests and backgrounds who respond to the things of the Lord in various ways. *Some* listen then immediately reject—instantly they turn it off. *Others* hear and seem to enjoy it and even respond well on the surface, but soon spin off when their bubble bursts and the going gets rough. Still others grab hold and initially embrace what they hear, but by and by they get sidetracked as their growth is throttled by life's "thorns." *Then*, as always, there are those who hear, believe, grow, hang in there and before long begin to reproduce as healthy plants in God's vineyard.

It's obvious that the first two groups are those who are *not* born-again. They are rootless, lifeless and fruitless. It's obvious that the last group *is* born-again:

submissive, active, and productive. But frankly, I'm bothered by the third group. They are Christians, because they grow and get right on the verge of bearing fruit, but their growth becomes retarded. The thorns which have grown up among them suffocate the normal healthy growth of each plant.

It is interesting that the thorns were already present at the time the seed entered, and that the thorns were never completely out of the picture even though the seed began to take root (Mark 4:7).

And what do the thorns represent? Again, we have Jesus' own words to answer that question. They represent "the worries of the world," "the deceitfulness of riches," and "the desires for other things" (4:19). When these thorns enter, spiritual growth and production slip out the rear exit. Our Lord doesn't say they *might* cause trouble, nor does He suggest they *have been known* to hinder us. He says that they . . . *enter in and choke the word, and it becomes unfruitful (v. 19)*.

Period. No ifs, ands, or maybes. The thorns are dictators. They know nothing of peaceful coexistence with the life of freedom and victory. Shunning the brash frontal attack characteristic of giant warfare, thorns employ a more subtle strategy. Slipping under the back door, their long tentacles advance so slowly, so silently, the victim hardly realizes he's being strangled. Demanding first place, they ultimately siphon off every ounce of spiritual interest and emotional energy.

Are you a compulsive worrier? Has the greenback made you greedy? Do you find it next to impossible to be satisfied with your present situation? If so, these words are nothing new to you—you've been stuck by those thorns since your soil first received God's seed . . . and if the truth were known, you inwardly enjoy their presence. After all, it's risky to abandon your entire life to God *by faith*. You'd rather worry, possess and complain, than rest, release and rejoice. Thorns inject a powerful anesthesia.

Why do so many Christians live among thorns? Because we have a quiet, respectable, secret *love* for them. I know. I've got the ugly scars to prove it. Each one is a mute reminder of years trapped in the thicket. And, periodically, I still have to yank a few.

I've never heard of such, but I'd like to proclaim today as Thorn Pulling Day. We may bleed and it may hurt . . . but, oh, the beauty of a thornless day!

Let's take a look at a few of the better-known thorns. Careful identification of these dangerous vines is the first step in clearing them from our gardens.

COMPARISON

If I may select a well-known phrase from the cobwebs of the 14th century and wipe away the dust to garner your attention, it is:

COMPARISONS ARE ODIOUS

Odious . . . disgusting, detestable. If you want to be a miserable mortal, then let the thorns of comparison run wild. You compare when you place someone beside someone else for the purpose of emphasizing the differences or showing the likenesses. This applies to places and things as well as people. We can become so proficient at this activity that we sustain our addiction through an unconscious force of habit. Inadvertently, the wheels of our thinking slide over into the ruts of this odious mindset. Comparison appears in at least two patterns.

Pattern one: We compare ourselves with others. You can imagine the results already. Either you are prompted to feel smug and proud because your strengths outweigh his weaknesses . . . or, more often, you begin to feel threatened, inferior and blue because you fail to measure up. Striving to emulate a self-imposed standard, you begin to slide from the pleasant plateau of the *real you* to the sinking sands of *I don't know who*. This sometimes leads to extreme role-playing where you try every way to adapt and alter your portrait to fit into someone else's frame. In simpler terms, you've pawned your real personality for a phony disguise. That's odious! Paul penned similar sentiments to a church that had become known for its comparison cliques:

We do not dare to classify or compare ourselves with those who commend themselves. When they measure themselves by themselves and compare themselves with themselves, they are not wise (2 Corinthinas 10:12 NIV).

The very next verse tells us, "Our goal is to measure up to God's plan *for us*" (TLB). Not for someone else, but for you, personally. God's great desire for us is that we fulfill His plan for us in our *own* lives. In His way—His timing.

Pattern two: We compare others with others. This is worse than unfair, it's stupid. And often cruel. Children suffer most from well-meaning adults who catalog one child's talents in front of another child in some misbegotten effort at motivation. "Look at your sister Debbie. If she can get an A in math, so can you." Or, "See how easy Jimmy learned to swim? Why are you so afraid?" That sort of comparison is toxic—poisoning a child's self-image and smothering the very motivation the parent was seeking to kindle.

But children aren't the only victims. People compare preachers and teachers, church philosophies and orders of service, soloists and song leaders, personalities and prayers, wives and mothers, families and friends, homes and cars, salaries and jobs, scholarship and salesmanship, husbands and fathers, weights and worries, luxuries and limitations, pain and pleasure. That's odious! Why not accept people and places and things *exactly as they are*? Isn't that true maturity? Why not accept and adjust to differences as quickly and enthusiastically as God forgives our wrongs and stands behind our efforts to try, try again? When love flows, acceptance grows.

Do you know what it is that kicks the slats out from under yesterday's routine and challenges us to rise and shine on today's menu of hours and minutes? It's *variety*. It's not the similarity of days that brings fresh motivation and stimulates enthusiasm—it's the lack of such, the varied *differences* that keep our attitudes positive and pleasing. To try and compare one day with another, then complain because today wasn't at all like yesterday, would be sheer folly and foolishness. The same principle applies to people.

Now listen very carefully: God, our wise and creative Maker, has been pleased to make everyone different and no one perfect. The sooner we appreciate and accept that fact, the deeper we will appreciate and accept one another, just as our Designer planned us. Actually, there is only one thing that would be worse than constant comparison, and that is if everyone were just alike. Can you think of anything more odious?

I can't.

"Striving to emulate a self-imposed standard, you begin to slide from the pleasant plateau of the real you to the sinking sands of I don't know who."

EXPECTATIONS

Battling thorns is a search-and-destroy process. Sometimes, however, the enemy eludes identification. They're tough to label. But I can think of at least two species which are easy to spot. That's because they almost always grow up together. Entwined from the roots up, these twin vines become practically inseparable. One is called *expectation*; the other is called *disappointment*.

Stop and think it over. What causes you to experience disappointment? Someone or something has failed to fulfill your expectations. Right? You had it all set up in your mind: the way a certain situation would work out, the way a certain person was going to respond. But it never materialized. Your wish fell fast and hard against stone-cold reality. Your desire dissolved into an empty, unfulfilled dream.

After you've heard a few stories of disappointment, they begin to sound painfully similar. As I spin some records in my memory, I hear several sad songs from different voices. Listen with me for a moment to their wistful echoes:

"I'm not happy in my work. When I got the job, I never realized it would be like this."

"Marriage has become a drag! On our wedding day I thought it would all be so different. It's nothing like I imagined at all."

"She was once a friend of mine. I reached out, helped her, loved her and gave myself to her. I thought the least she would do was respond the same way to me."

"We had them over for dinner more than once and they never did reciprocate. We didn't even get a thank-you note. Talk about a disappointment!"

"He asked me out several times. I felt I was more than just another date to him. I really anticipated a deepening romance . . . but it never occurred. I was hurt."

"Man, I chose this college thinking it would provide me with an ideal education. Now here I am a senior—but I'm not nearly as prepared as I thought I would be."

"The discipleship group was nothing like I expected. I anticipated one thing and got another."

"We came to this church with high hopes. Expecting great things, we threw ourselves into the program without reservation. Now we're disillusioned with the whole thing."

"Glad we had children? Hardly. You know, we thought having kids was going to be fun—a downhill slide. You can't imagine how happy we are to see them leave the nest. They really let us down."

"God called me into the ministry. He later led my family and me into the pastorate. We were burning with zeal and bursting with hope. But after ten years, the fire's gone out. The delight just isn't there anymore. I'm frustrated."

"Yeah, we just got back from Europe. No, it wasn't that great. Nothing like we thought it would be."

Recognize the tune? The scratchy sounds on the disappointment side of the disc are well-worn. Self-made bitterness, resentment and pessimism ooze from the grooves. It's played year after year and we've all heard it—or sung it.

It's time we switched to the flip-side. We need to take an honest look at this painful thorn that blurs our vision and conceives our disappointments. *Expectations.* We erect mental images which are either unrealistic, unfair or biased. Those phantom images become our inner focus, rigidly and traditionally maintained. Leaving no room for flexibility on the part of the other person (allowing no place for circumstantial change or surprise) we set in mental concrete *the way* things must go. When they *don't*, we either tumble or grumble . . . or both.

The result is tragic. As our radius of toleration is reduced, our willingness to accept others' imperfections or a less-than-ideal circumstance is short-circuited. And, worst of all, the delightful spontaneity of a friendship is strained. The chain of obligation, built with the links of expectation, binds us in the dungeon of disappointment.

With all due respect to the beloved hymn we've sung half our lives, I'd suggest we change the title to "Blest Be the Tie that *Frees*."

We need to give one another stretching space—the room to respond and react in a variety of ways, even as our infinite Creator molded a variety of personalities.

This will require a ritual burning of our list of expectations. For some of us, it could make quite a bonfire. It will also mean we stop anticipating the *ideal* and start living with the real—which is always checkered with failure, imperfection and even *wrong*. So instead of biting and devouring one another (à la Galatians 5:15), let's support individual freedom as we serve one another in love (à la Galatians 5:13).

Get a firm grip on the weed of expectation and you'll uproot your disappointment at the same time. Two thorns with one pull. That's a bargain.

PESSIMISM

A person is the product of his own thoughts. Thoughts form the thermostat which regulates what we accomplish in life. My body responds and reacts to the input from my mind. If I feed my mind with doubt, worry and discouragement, that is precisely the kind of day I will experience. If I adjust my thermostat forward—to thoughts filled with vision, hope and victory—I can count on *that* kind of day. You and I become what we *think* about.

Take a minute to give your imagination a workout. Consider your mind a factory—a busy, bustling workshop of action and production. That's not far from the truth. Your mind is a *thought* factory. Every day on that internal assembly line it produces thousands, perhaps *hundreds* of thousands of thoughts. Production in your thought factory is under the charge of two foremen. The names on their hardhats are Mr. Gainground and Mr. Slideback. Mr. Gainground, as you'd imagine, oversees the production of positive thoughts. At the pull of a lever, wholesome, encouraging, reassuring plans and positive ideas roll down the belt and into the showroom.

That other foreman, Mr. Slideback, has responsibilities too. Over in a darker, damp wing of the plant, Gainground's counterpart manufactures negative, depreciating, worrisome thoughts. Both foremen are well qualified for their respective duties. Gainground specializes in producing reasons why you can face life triumphantly, why you can handle whatever comes your way, why you're more than a conqueror. Old Slideback earned his Masters at Inadequate U. He's full of reasons why you cannot succeed, why you're pitifully unable, why you should cave in, bow down and surrender to the tangled thicket of inferiority, failure and discouragement.

Both foremen, however, are instantly obedient. They await your signal to snap to attention. Provide yourself with a positive signal and Mr. Gainground throws himself into action. Pulling all the right switches, Gainground so gears production that one encouraging, edifying thought after another floods your mind and fills your life. As long as production is under his firm control, not even the slightest mist of misgiving may be observed hovering under the factory ceiling.

Foreman Slideback, however, awaits a negative signal (which he would prefer to call "reality" or "common sense") and he's off and running. At peak production, Slideback's assembly line cranks out discouraging, bad-news thoughts faster than the mind can process them. He will soon have you convinced that you *can't* or *won't* or *shouldn't*. Given sufficient time, he will drain your energy, squelch your confidence and transform you into a frowning, tight-lipped fatalist.

Neither Dale Carnegie nor Norman Vincent Peale originated such a message as this—God did. Listen to three Biblical counselors:

Solomon, referring to attitudes: *For as he thinks within himself, so he is* (Proverbs 23:7).

Paul, referring to thoughts: *Finally, brethren, whatever is true, whatever is honorable, whatever is right, whatever is pure, whatever is lovely, whatever is of good repute . . . let your mind dwell on these things* (Philippians 4:8).

Peter, referring to the mind: *Therefore, gird your minds for action* (1 Peter 1:13).

Thoughts, positive or negative, grow stronger when fertilized with constant repetition. That may explain why so many who are gloomy and gray stay in that mood, and why others who are cheery and enthusiastic continue to be so, even in the midst of difficult circumstances. Please do not misunderstand. Happiness (like winning) is a matter of right thinking, not intelligence, age or position. Our performance is directly related to the thoughts we deposit in our memory bank. We can only draw on what we deposit.

What kind of performance would your car deliver if every morning before you left for work you scooped up a handful of dirt and put it in your crankcase? The fine-tuned engine would soon be coughing and sputtering. Ultimately, it would refuse to start. The same is true of your life. Thoughts about yourself and attitudes toward others that are narrow, destructive and abrasive produce wear and tear on your mental motor. They send you off the road while others drive past.

You need only one foreman in your factory. The name is Mr. Gainground and he's anxious to assist you. In fact, he is immediately available to all the members of God's family. His real name is the Holy Spirit—the Helper. If Mr. Slideback has been too busily engaged as foreman on your mental assembly line, then—*fire yours and hire ours*! You'll be astounded by how smoothly the plant will run under His leadership.

HABITS

I used to bite my fingernails right down to the quick. I'd rip off those babies just as soon as the first signs of new growth would appear. For well over 20 years I carried around ten ugly stumps which resulted in two miserable experiences:

1. *Personal embarrassment.* I was always afraid of such things as "clean hands inspection" at school and summer camps. And doctor's exams where the man would look down and groan at my mitts.

2. *Physical limitations.* If I ever dropped a dime—*forget it*! The same for trying to pick up a toothpick, pluck out splinters, or put in tiny screws. My mom tried all sorts of gimmicks to make me stop: money bribes, red-hot-burn-your-mouth-stuff painted on my nails, wearing gloves day and night, public embarrassment and private reminders. But nothing worked, and I mean *nothing*. I'd go right on and bite them off until they'd bleed. I remember having dates and keeping my hands in my pockets the whole time so the girl wouldn't notice. I avoided card games, skipped piano lessons, refused to try on rings and stayed away from handcraft projects. How I hated that habit! I wanted so badly to stop I would stay awake at night thinking about it. But the simple fact was *I couldn't*. In spite of the pain and the pressure, that habit, like all habits, had me in its grip.

As the American educator, Horace Mann, once described the predicament: *Habit is a cable; we weave a thread of it every day, and at last we cannot break it.*

But God began to convict me about my nail-nibbling ways. It took Him nearly a decade to bring about a final and complete victory, ashamed as I am to admit it. During the process He gently, yet pointedly, caused me to see that this was an area of my life much deeper than eight fingers and a couple thumbs. I was being enslaved—mastered and manipulated by the thorny vines of habit. I was a living contradiction to the liberating truth of 1 Corinthians 6:12:

> *All things are lawful for me, but not all things are profitable. All things are lawful for me, but I will not be mastered by anything.*

You can't believe the fire of conviction this verse once set ablaze within me. The Greek word translated "mastered" means "to be held under the authority of something." A close look reveals that this isn't a verse talking about something lawless or wicked, but something that is actually *lawful . . . but not profitable*. My first encounter with the verse was not my final encounter with this painful habit. But it was certainly a turning point toward change, thank God.

The backwash of this nail-biting testimony has far-reaching effects. Not a person who reads this book is completely free from bad habits, whether lawless or lawful. That's the price we pay for being human. Some are wrestling with a habit as accepted and common as overeating or exaggerating or cheating or procrastinating. Others, by habit, are negative and suspicious, resulting in habitually closeminded responses. While some are ungrateful and demanding, others are continually extravagant and undiscerning.

Some of you feel trapped by overt dependence on alcohol consumption, addiction to drugs, cravings for nicotine and caffeine, the lure of sensual lust or a pill for every ill. Habits like gossip, worry, irritability and profanity are often practiced without guilt, justified through cleverly-devised mental schemes. The list is endless, for habits are as numerous as every detail of life. Rather than enlarging the list, let's focus on five suggestions that may help yank out some of these thorns that hinder our walk.

Stop rationalizing. Refuse to make comments like: "Oh, that's just me. I'm just like that—always have been, always will be. After all, nobody's perfect." Such excuses take the edge off disobedience and encourage you to diminish or completely ignore the Spirit's work of conviction.

Apply strategy. Approach your target with a rifle, not a shotgun. Take on each habit one at a time, not all at once.

Be realistic. It won't happen fast. It won't be easy. Nor will your resolve be permanent overnight. Periodic failures, however, are still better than habitual slavery.

Be encouraged. Realize you're on the road to ultimate triumph . . . for the first time in years! Enthusiasm strengthens self-discipline and prompts an attitude of stick-to-itiveness.

Start today. This is the very best moment thus far in your life. To put it off is an admission of defeat and will only intensify and prolong your losing the self-confidence battle.

Extracting the hurtful thorns of habit enables the pilgrim to focus less attention on himself and more attention on the One who is worthy. And the most exciting thought of all is that He will be right there in the morning ready to help you through the day with all the power you will need, one moment at a time.

Need proof? How about ten fingernails and an emery board?

"The chains of habit are too small to be felt until they are too strong to be broken."
—Benjamin R. Dejung

CLICHES

I'd like to start a club. But not just any club. I've had the name and membership requirements for this particular organization tattooed on the underside of my eyelids for a long time.

It's going to be called a *DWAC Club:* Down With All Clichés! Getting in won't be easy. In order to become a member, you'll have to pledge yourself to a life of verbal discipline. You'll have to promise a bold breakout from the penitentiary of worn-out expressions where you've been imprisoned for too many years.

But that's not all. You will also have to promise to express yourself in fresh, penetrating ways to both God and fellow man. Before getting in line to join DWAC, let me warn you: The dues are high. *First*, you will have to put the torch to much of your "spiritual language," throwing into the bonfire your treasured list of pet expressions. *Second*, you will be required to stretch your mental muscles as you force yourself to substitute meaningful terms in place of religious-sounding ad lib.

Still want to sign up? A *third* bylaw insists that you learn to adjust to a world free from the security of such threadbare clichés as:

"... lead, guide and direct us ..."
"... may the Lord add His blessing to the reading of His Word ..."
"... I trust this will be a blessing to your heart and life ..." (yawn)
"... just trust the Lord ..."
"... share my testimony ..."
"... bless all the missionaries ..."
"... we thank Thee for everything ..."
"... it will all work together for good ..."
"... wonderful message in song ..." (sigh)
"... bless the gift and the giver ..."
"... shall we bow our hearts together? ..."

". . . a time of food, fun, and fellowship . . ." (zzzz)
". . . bless this food to our bodies . . ."
". . . gone on to glory . . ."
. . . ad infinitum, AD NAUSEUM!

Now wait—stop and think before you pick up stones to stone me. Haven't you heard those weather-beaten phrases so long you could scream? Or worse—maybe you're so mesmerized or embalmed that you don't even hear them anymore. Christians seem to have developed the use of trite, hackneyed words and phrases into an art. *Cliché* is a French term, really. Originally, it meant "stereotype," and Mr. Webster defines stereotype: "To repeat without variation; frequent and almost mechanical repetition of the same thing . . . something conforming to a fixed pattern." Like a broken record . . . a pull-string doll with ten pre-recorded phrases . . . the ceaseless droning of parking regulations at an airport.

Our Lord once told the Pharisees they were guilty of using "meaningless repetition" when they prayed (Matthew 6:7). *Don't we?* Are we qualified to sit in judgment? On another occasion Jesus rebuked them for appearing and sounding righteous before men when they were inwardly full of hypocrisy (Matthew 23:27-28). All right, which one of us is going to cast the first stone at those Pharisees?

Without wanting to sound like an ultra-critical heretic, I will name a few places where 20th-century clichés abound:

- In stale, cranked-out testimonies, lacking relevance and fresh thinking.
- In public prayers, particularly in groups where we "take turns" around the circle, or in pastoral and pre-offering prayers.
- In religious radio and television broadcasts, especially when the announcer or preacher is unprepared, lapsing into his shopworn stock of religious jargon.
- In old sermons warmed over in late Saturday night's oven, served the next morning.
- In missions conferences, Bible conferences, men's conferences, couples' conferences, prophetic conferences, family life conferences, most all conferences!
- In answers to standard questions about God, the Bible and doubtful things.
- In pat, "doctrinal advice" to the sick, sinful and sorrowing.

- In weddings and funerals.
- In lengthy devotionals tacked on at the end of a "fun" gathering.
- In public announcements made during "opening exercises" (cliché!) and church services.
- In seasonal greetings at Christmas, Easter, Mother's Day, Groundhog Day, etc.
- In cranked-out invocations and benedictions.

Honestly, I am not condemning. *I am pleading.*

We are witnesses and spokesmen for the God of infinite variety, boundless creativity, indescribable majesty and beauty. We hold in our possession a white-hot message of hope, a pulsating invitation to approach a living Saviour. Can we justify garbing this hope in faded sackcloth, delivering it in a predictable monotone? I am longing for those of us afflicted with anemic phraseology to step forward for a transfusion. I am asking for a frank admission that our assembly-line answers and stale statements are covered with the cobweb of tradition spun by the spider of laziness. Many of our words lost their impact years ago, suffering for decades from the public abuse of overuse. The thorns have budded, blossomed and reproduced until they've hedged out light and fresh air.

Before five separate groups, one after another, Paul described his life and service for the Great King. Yet each time he stayed creative. You won't find a single cliché in the inspired record of the battered apostle's words (Acts 22-26). If Paul could do it, so should we.

At this point, I openly submit a confession. *Preachers are the worst offenders.* If $5 fines were issued for each cliché that escapes over the pulpit, most of us would be broke at the end of each month. So let's sign a pact together, and call it a mutual DWAC project, okay? I will do everything in my power to tune up my communications . . . if you will, too. Let's fumigate our phrases, destroying forever that plague of verbal locusts which threatens to consume the vitality and freshness of our all-important message.

All potential DWAC clubbers: sign that membership card today. I've got my pen out, too.

SUPERSTITION

The great plague stretched across the Old Country like a thick, drab blanket. It came as a thief in the night . . . unannounced, treacherous, silent. Before it left, 25 million people on the Isles and in Europe had died. The mortality rate was astounding. In May of 1664, a few isolated cases were reported and quietly ignored. Exactly one year later, 590 died that month. By June it was 6,137; July, over 17,000; August, over 31,000. Panic struck. More than two-thirds of the remaining population fled from their homes to escape death.

It was called *Black Death* for two reasons:

1. The body of the victim became dark, black splotches covering the skin.

2. The blackness of ignorance surrounded its cause. Because of this, no cure was known.

Someone came up with the foolish idea that polluted air brought on the plague. So, people began to carry flower petals in their pockets, superstitiously thinking the fragrance would ward off the disease. Groups of victims, if they were able to walk, were taken outside the hospitals. Holding hands, they walked in circles around rose gardens, breathing in deeply the aroma of the blooming plants. In some cases, the patient couldn't get out of bed, so the attending physicians filled their pockets with bright-colored petals from English posy plants. While visiting the patient they walked around the bed sprinkling the posy petals on and around the victim.

As death came closer, another superstitious act was employed with sincerity. Many felt if the lungs could be freed from pollution, life could be sustained. So, ashes were placed in a spoon and brought up near the nose, causing a hefty sneeze or two. But neither flowers nor sneezes retarded the raging death rate. Not until the real cause was discovered—the bite of fleas from diseased rats—was the plague brought in check.

The awful experience gave birth to a little song which innocent children still sing at play. It was first heard from the lips of a soiled, old man pushing a cart in London, picking up bodies along an alley:

"Superstition, although prompted by sincerity, brings the plague of slavery. Sincerity doesn't liberate; Christ does."

Ring around the roses,
A pocket full of posies;
Ashes, ashes, We all fall down.

Conceived in the mind by ignorance, superstition cultivates insecurity and sends a legion of structural cracks through our character. It feeds on exaggerated, self-made lies which grow so thick that the boughs hide common sense and, worse, God.

You find superstition in sports. Some basketball players testify they simply cannot play the game unless they go through their strange warm-up ritual. The manager of one professional baseball team doesn't dare stop on a white baseline. Several pro football running backs have superstitious "dances" that follow their touchdowns—and you better not try to stop them! An Olympic runner several years ago admitted he has to rub the medal that hangs around his neck, or he can't get properly "psyched up." One of America's Olympic skiers, the news media reported, sticks a four-leaf clover in her jacket pocket before she hits the slopes.

Superstition enslaves many an entertainer. You wouldn't believe the mental contortions they go through before their performances. Students are superstitious about getting good grades. The elderly are superstitious about their safety at home. Mothers are superstitious about their babies at night. Men are superstitious about their success in sales, or the future of their careers. Multiplied millions are superstitious about their astrological forecast.

The worst? Superstition regarding the Lord God. The Reformers were among the first to see it and call a spade a spade. They wrote of it, preached against it, publicly exposed it—and were martyred because of it. Religious superstition is ruthless.

Before you write this off as applying to anyone but yourself, take a long hard look at your own life. The goal of superstition is *bondage*. Remember that. It's why superstition is counted among the thorns of life. If *anything* in your Christianity has you in bondage, it is probable that superstition is the breeding ground. You see, our Saviour came to give us the truth and set us free. Superstition, although prompted by sincerity, brings the plague of slavery. Sincerity doesn't liberate; Christ does.

You may be sincere. As sincere as a pocketful of petals or a spoonful of ashes or a song in the alley. But what good is a song if it's sung to a corpse?

77

BUSYNESS

Run, saint run!
Appointments, activities, assignments . . . run!
Demands, decisions, deadlines . . . run!
Schedules, services, seminars . . . run!
Plans, programs, people . . .
Stop!

Step aside and sit down. Let your motor idle down for a minute and think for a change. Think about your pace . . . your busyness. How did you get trapped in that squirrel cage? What is it down inside your boiler room that keeps pouring the coal on your fire? Caught your breath yet? Take a glance back over your shoulder, say, three or four months. Could you list anything significant accomplished? How about feelings of fulfillment—very many? Probably not, if you're honest.

There's a man in Oklahoma City named James Sullivan who knows how you feel. Back in the 1960s he blew his town wide open developing the largest Young Life Club in the nation. And that's not all he blew wide open. Along the way, he managed to sacrifice his health and his family. Blazing along the success track, Sullivan became a difficult man to keep up with, let alone live with. His wife, Carolyn, was getting tired. So were his children, who seldom saw their father. When they did, he was irritable. Although he never realized it at the time, Sullivan's full-throttle lifestyle was actually an escape technique. Listen to his admission in his book, *The Frog Who Never Became a Prince*:

> *I was a man who existed in a shell . . . guilt, resentment, and hatred welled up within me. The resulting hard feelings I developed became almost insurmountable.*

What happened? Wasn't this guy a Christian, working for Jesus, spreading the Gospel, reaching the youth? Yes, indeed. But Sullivan substituted activity for living, busyness for meaningful priorities. One Thanksgiving Carolyn asked him a question as he was racing out the door to speak at some camp. "Do you know," she said, "or do you even care, that from the middle of September until today, you have not been home *one* night?" Not long after that, she broke emotionally. He contemplated suicide.

STINGING WORDS—BUT TRUE. SOUND FAMILIAR? HERE'S WHY:

Busyness rapes relationships. It substitutes shallow frenzy for deep friendship. It promises satisfying dreams but delivers hollow nightmares. It feeds the ego but starves the inner man. It fills a calendar but fractures a family. It cultivates a program but plows under priorities.

Many a church boasts about its active program: "Something every night of the week for everybody." What a shame! With good intentions the local assembly can *create* the very atmosphere it was designed to curb. The One who instructed us to "be still and know that I am God" must hurt when He witnesses our frantic, compulsive, agitated motions. In place of a quiet, responsive spirit we offer Him an inner washing machine—churning with anxiety, clogged with too much activity and spilling over with resentment and impatience. Sometimes He must watch our convulsions with a heavy sigh.

My mentor was wise. He once declared:

Much of our activity these days is nothing more than a cheap anesthetic to deaden the pain of an empty life.

SEARCHING WORDS—BUT TRUE. WANT TO CHANGE? HERE'S HOW:

First, *admit it.* You are too busy. Say it to yourself . . . your family . . . your friends. Openly and willingly *acknowledge* that what you are doing is wrong and something must be done—now. I did that recently and, through tears, my family and I cleared some bridges the thorns had overgrown.

Second, *stop it.* Starting today, refuse every possible activity which isn't absolutely necessary. Sound ruthless? So is the clock. So is your health. Start saying "No." Practice saying it aloud a few times—form the letters in your mouth. The phonetic structure of this two-letter word really isn't all that difficult. If feasible, resign from a committee or two . . . or three or four. Quit feeling so important. They'll get somebody else. Or maybe they'll wise up and adopt a better plan.

Third, *maintain it.* It's easy to start fast and fade quickly. Discuss with your family some ways of investing time with *them*—without the TV . . . without apologies for playing and laughing and doing nutty, fun things . . . without gobs of money having to be spent to ''entertain'' you.

Fourth, *share it*. It won't be very long before you begin gleaning the benefits of putting first things first. Tell others. Infect them with some germs of your excitement. Believe me, there are a lot of activity-addicts within the fellowship of faith who'd love to stop running . . . if they only knew how.

Ask James Sullivan. His nickname is ''Frog.'' By the time he got kissed, it was almost too late.

Almost.

"There are a lot of activity addicts who'd love to stop running . . . if they only knew how."

EROSION

I remember only two things from my high school chemistry class. First, I got rid of a wart on the back of my right hand through applications of sulfuric acid for 33 consecutive days. Second, I watched the slow death of a frog in an unforgettable experiment.

My teacher placed the hapless creature in an oversized beaker of cool water. Beneath the beaker he moved a Bunsen burner with a very low flame so that the water heated very slowly—something like .017 of a degree Fahrenheit per second. In fact, the temperature rose so gradually that the frog was never aware of the change. Two and a half hours later the frog was dead . . . *boiled to death*. The change occurred so slowly that the frog neither tried to jump out nor released a complaining kick.

Attentive as I was to the gruesome demonstration, I never realized I was witnessing a profound principle that would remind me of that frog for the rest of my life. The principle, in a word, is *erosion* . . . the silent toll of deterioration.

The first eleven chapters of 1 Kings record the erosion of a great man, in fact, *the* greatest of his day. Blessed with royal blood and an abundance of brains, Solomon was a natural for the throne of David. As the heir-apparent, he was tutored at the feet of Nathan, groomed through the heart of Bathsheba, polished under the eyes of David, and matured by the hand of God. The mark of excellence was upon him. Though he was young when his father died, he was thoroughly prepared to take the scepter and reign over Israel.

Wisdom, loyalty, diplomacy, faithfulness and efficiency characterized the attitudes and acts of David's gifted son for the first few years of his kingship. Best of all, "Solomon loved the Lord" (1 Kings 3:3) and carefully walked in His ways. His achievements, power, international influence and wealth were nothing short of phenomenal:

> *Now God gave Solomon wisdom and very great discernment and breadth of*
> *mind, like the sand that is on the seashore. And Solomon's wisdom surpassed the*

wisdom of all the sons of the east and all the wisdom of Egypt. For he was wiser than all men . . . and his fame was known in all the surrounding nations . . . So King Solomon became greater than all the kings of the earth in riches and in wisdom . . . And all the earth was seeking the presence of Solomon (1 Kings 4:29-31, 10:23-24a).

It has been proven that his annual income reached well into the millions. The unparalleled achievement of his life was the design and construction of Solomon's Temple, one of the seven wonders of the ancient world. After the suspicious queen of Sheba came to visit his kingdom to satisfy her mind that all she had heard was not merely an exaggeration, she humbly admitted:

. . . I did not believe the reports, until I came and my eyes had seen it. And behold, the half was not told me. You exceed in wisdom and prosperity the report which I heard (1 Kings 10:7).

Candidly, Solomon had it all.

Things slowly began to change, however. Almost as if he had attained the mastery of man and God, he seized the reigns of compromise and wrong, and drove himself to the misty flats of licentiousness, pride, lust and idolatry. Like insane Nero in later history, Solomon became irrational, sensual and even skeptical of things he once held precious.

Layers of dust collected in the majestic temple he had built, now that the monarch had turned his attention to another project: the building of strange edifices for the strange gods he and his strange wives were now serving. Solomon (like many another absolute monarch, super salesman, top business executive, athletic prima donna, or filmstar playboy) simply drove too fast and traveled too far. The vultures of his own vulnerability soon spotted his carnal carcass and began to feed upon his vitals. The termination of his now sterile life came prematurely. His so-called "success story" now stank.

The son of David died a debauched, effeminate cynic, so satiated with materialism that life was all "vanity and striving after wind" (Ecclesiastes 2:26b). He left a nation confused, in conflict and soon to be fractured by civil war.

Deterioration is never sudden. No garden "suddenly" overgrows with thorns. No church "suddenly" splits. No building "suddenly" crumbles. No tree "suddenly" falls. No marriage "suddenly" breaks down. No nation "suddenly" becomes a mediocre power. No person "suddenly" becomes base. Slowly, almost imperceptibly, certain things are accepted that once were rejected. Things once considered hurtful are now secretly tolerated. At the outset it appears harmless, perhaps even exciting, but the wedge it brings leaves a gap that grows wider as moral erosion joins hands with spiritual decay. The gap becomes a canyon. That "way which seems right" becomes, in fact, "the way of death." Solomon wrote that. He ought to know.

Take heed, you who stand: take heed, lest *you* fall! Be careful about changing your standard so that it corresponds with your desires. Be very cautious about becoming inflated with thoughts of your own importance. Be alert to the pitfalls of prosperity and success. Should God grant riches, fame and success, don't run scared or feel guilty. Just stay balanced. Remember Solomon, who deteriorated from a humble man of wisdom to a vain fool in a rather brief span of time.

I'm now grateful for that chemistry class experiment I witnessed back in 1951. At the time I kept thinking, "What a drag." No longer. The memory of that frog has kept me out of a lot of hot water.

APPREHENSION

The scene is familiar: a hospital lobby with all the trimmings . . . soft sofas and folded newspapers . . . matching carpets and drapes illumined by eerie lighting . . . an uniformed lady at the desk weary from answering the same questions . . . strange smells . . . ash trays half full of half-finished smokes . . . and people.

Everywhere there are *people*. A steady stream pours in and out, the faces marked by hurry and worry. Surrounding me are small clusters of coffee-sipping groups talking quietly or looking into space, blinking often, lost in a world of their own anguish. Some sit alone, restlessly studying the same page of a paperback for ten minutes. A surgeon in faded green garb suddenly appears, bearing news to the waiting. Frowns cut in. Lips tighten. Heads shake. Tears flow. Everyone stares—momentarily identifying with the strangers. Soon it's quiet again, increased apprehension mounts . . . and life goes on.

If I were a bug on the wall of this sterile establishment, I'd remember other places I'd clung to and sensed apprehension in my insect excursions. Like the classroom observing the new teacher on her first attempt with junior high schoolers. Like the cramped study of the final-year med student as he crams the night before his orals. I'd recall the apprehension I saw at the airport as a dad waved goodbye to his son leaving for overseas duty. Or in the nursery as an exhausted mother sat through the night beside her baby with a raging fever. Or the time I landed on the window of a car traveling cross-country, moving a family to an unfamiliar neighborhood with unknown streets and untried challenges. Or the store owned by the businessman who was squeezed in the inflation vise and didn't see how he could make payroll on the first.

Apprehension. It's as American as a Chevy V-8 or TV dinners. And it's strange. Apprehension is a notch or two above worry, but it feels like its twin. It isn't strong enough to be fear, but neither is it mild enough to be funny. It's in the category of a "mixed emotion."

(You know, of course, the definition of mixed emotions. It's the feeling you get when you hear the news that your mother-in-law just drove your new Mercedes 450 SEL over the cliff. You really don't know whether to look shocked or relieved, so you wind your watch, look down at the ground, sigh and pray for wisdom.)

In some ways, apprehension leaves you crippled, immobile. It's an undefined uneasiness—a feeling of uncertainty, misgiving and unrest. What frustration is to yesterday, apprehension is to tomorrow.

Paul had it when he set his face toward the heavy horizon over Jerusalem. His admission is found in Acts 20:22:

> *And now, behold, bound in spirit, I am on my way to Jerusalem, not knowing what will happen to me there.*

A lot of emotion was packed into those 21 words. How did he feel? *Bound in spirit.* Why was he uneasy? *Not knowing what will happen to me.* That's the thorn of apprehension. It is no sin. Nor is it reason for embarrassment. Rather, it is proof positive that you're human. Unfortunately, it tends to smother your pleasant dreams by placing a pillow over your faith. Apprehension will strap a short leash on your vision and teach you to roll over and play dead when scary statistics and pessimistic reports snap their fingers.

Paul absolutely refused to run when it whistled at him. Openly acknowledging its presence, he nevertheless stood his ground with the ringing words of Acts 20:24:

> *But I do not consider my life of any account as dear to myself, in order that I may finish my course, and the ministry which I received from the Lord Jesus . . . .*

Apprehension is impressive until determination pulls rank on it and forces it to salute. This is especially true when determination has been commissioned by the King of kings.

IMPATIENCE

As I write this I'm at 35,000 feet. It's 5:45 p.m., Saturday. It should be 4:15. The airliner was an hour and a half late. People are grumpy. Some are downright mad. Stewardesses are apologizing, promising extra booze to take off the edge. To complicate matters, a Japanese man across the aisle from me has a rather severe nosebleed and they're trying to instruct the poor chap . . . *but he doesn't speak a word of English*!

So now the meal is late. The lady on my left has a cold and makes an enormous sound when she sneezes (about every 90 seconds—I've timed her). It's something like a dying calf in a hail storm or a bull moose with one leg in a trap. Oh, one more thing. The sports film on golf just broke down and so did the nervous systems of half the men on board. It's a zoo!

It all started with the *delay*. "Mechanical trouble," they said. "Inexcusable," responded a couple of passengers. Frankly, I'd rather they fix it before we leave than decide to do something about it en route. But we Americans don't like to wait. Delays are irritating. Aggravating. Nerve-jangling. With impatient predictability we are consistently—and I might add *obnoxiously*—demanding. We want what we want *when* we want it. Not a one of us finds a delay easy to accept.

Do you question that? Put yourself into these situations:

• You're at the grocery store. Busy evening ahead. Long lines. Shopping cart has a wheel that drags. You finally finish and choose a stall with only two ahead of you. The checker is new on the job . . . her hands tremble . . . beads of perspiration dot her brow. Slowly she gets to you. Her cash register tape runs out. She isn't sure how to change it. You're delayed. How's your response?

• It's dinner-out-with-the-family night. That special place. You've fasted most of the day so you can gorge tonight. You're given a booth and a menu but the place is terribly busy and two waitresses short. So there you sit, hungry as a buffalo in winter with a glass of water and a menu you've begun to gnaw on. You're delayed. How's your response?

• You're a little late to work. The freeway's full so you decide to slip through traffic using a rarely-known shortcut only Daniel Boone could have figured out. You hit all green lights as you slide around trucks and slow drivers. Just about the time you start feeling foxy, an ominous clang, clang, clang strikes your ears. A train! You're delayed. How's your response?

The rubber of Christianity meets the road of proof at just such intersections in life. As the expression goes, our faith is "fleshed out" at times like that. The best test of my Christian growth occurs in the mainstream of life, not in the quietness of my study. *Anybody* can walk in victory when surrounded by books, silence and the warm waves of sunshine splashing through the window. But those late takeoffs, those grocery lines, those busy restaurants, those trains! What fertilizer for the thorns of impatience!

The stewardess on this plane couldn't care less that I'm a pretribulational rapturist. Your waitress will not likely be impressed that you can prove the authorship of the Pentateuch. Nor will the gal at the checkstand stare in awe as you inform her of the distinctive characteristics of Biblical infallibility which you embrace (although she *may* stare).

One quality, however—a single, rare virtue scarce as diamonds and twice as precious—will immediately attract them to you and soften their spirits. That quality? The ability to accept delay graciously. Calmly. Quietly. Understandingly. With a smile. If the robe of purity is far above rubies, the garment of patience is even beyond that. Why? Because its threads of unselfishness and kindness are woven in the Lord's loom, guided within our lives by the Spirit of God. But, alas, the garment seldom clothes us!

Remember the verse?

But the fruit of the Spirit is love, joy, peace . . .

And what else? The first three are the necessary style along with the buttons and zipper of the garment. The rest give it color and beauty:

. . . patience, kindness, goodness, faithfulness, gentleness, self-control. . . .

The ability to accept delay. Or disappointment. To smile back at setbacks and respond with a pleasant, understanding spirit. To cool it while others around you curse it. For a change, I refused to be hassled by today's delay. I asked God to keep me calm and cheerful, relaxed and refreshed. Know what? He did. He *really* did!

No pills. No booze. No hocus-pocus. Just relaxing in the power of Jesus.

I can't promise you that others will understand. You see, I've got another problem now. Ever since takeoff I've been smiling at the stewardesses, hoping to encourage them. Just now I overheard one of them say to the other, "Watch that guy wearing glasses. I think he's had too much to drink."

PHARISAISM

Jesus opened a five-gallon can of worms the day He preached His sermon on the mount. There wasn't a Pharisee within gunshot range who wouldn't have given his last denarius to see Him strung up by sundown. Did they hate Him! They hated Him because He refused to let them get away with their phony religious drool and their super-spiritual ooze that was polluting the public.

The Messiah unsheathed His sharp sword of truth the day He ascended the mountain. When He came down that evening, it was dripping with the blood of hypocrites. If ever an individual exposed pride, Jesus did that day. His words bit into their hides like harpoons into whale blubber. Never in their notorious, smug careers had they been pierced with such deadly accuracy. Like bloated beasts of the deep they floated to the surface for all to see.

If there was one thing Jesus despised, it was the very thing every Pharisee majored in at seminary: showing off, or, to cushion it a bit, self-righteousness. They were the Holy Joes of Palestine, the first to enlist undiscerning recruits into the Royal Order of Back-Stabbers. They were past-masters in the practice of put-down prayers, and spent their days working on ways to impress others with their somber expression and monotonous, dismal drone. Worst of all, by sowing the seeds of legalistic thorns and nurturing them into forbidding vines of religious intolerance, the Pharisees prevented honest seekers from approaching their God.

Even today, the thorns of legalism spread a paralyzing poison into the Body of Christ. The venom blinds our eyes, dulls our edge and arouses pride in our hearts. Soon our love is eclipsed as it turns into a mental clipboard with a long checklist, a thick filter requiring others to measure up before we move in. The joy of friendship is fractured by a judgmental attitude and a critical look. It seems stupid to me that fellowship must be limited to the narrow ranks of predictable personalities clad in "acceptable" attire. The short haircut, clean-shaven, tailored suit look (with matching vest and tie, of course), seem essential in many circles. Just because I prefer a certain style or attire doesn't mean that it's best or that it's for everyone. Nor does it mean that the opposite is any *less* pleasing to God.

Our problem is a gross intolerance of those who don't fit *our* mold—an attitude which reveals itself in the stoic stare or a caustic comment. Such legalistic and prejudiced reactions will thin the ranks of the local church faster than fire in the basement or flu in the pew. If you question that, take a serious look at the Galatians letter. Paul's pen flowed with heated ink as he rebuked them for "deserting" Christ (1:6), "nullifying the grace of God" (2:21), becoming "be-witched" by legalism (3:1), and desiring "to be enslaved" by this crippling disease (4:9).

Sure . . . there are limits to our freedom. Grace *does not* condone license. Love has its Biblical restrictions. The opposite of legalism is not "do as you please." But listen! The limitations are far broader than most of us realize. I can't believe, for example, that the only music God smiles on is highbrow or hymns. Why not country-folk or Dixieland as well? Nor do I believe the necessary garment for entering the Veil is a suit and tie. Why won't cutoffs or jeans and Hang Ten tee-shirts do just as well? Shocked? Let's remember who it is that becomes wrought-up over outward appearances. Certainly not God!

> . . . *God sees not as man sees, for man looks at the outward appearance, but the*
> *Lord looks at the heart (1 Samuel 16:7b).*

And who can prove that the only voice God will bless is the ordained minister on Sunday? How about the salesman Tuesday afternoon or the high school teacher Friday morning?

It is helpful to remember that our Lord reserved His strongest and longest sermon not for struggling sinners, discouraged disciples, or even prosperous people, but for hypocrites, glory hogs, legalists—the present-day Pharisees.

The message on the mountain delivered that afternoon centuries ago echoes down the canyons of time with pristine force and clarity.

Listen to Matthew 6:1:

> *Beware of practicing your righteousness before men to be noticed by them . . .*

In other words, stop showing off! Stop looking down your nose at others who don't fill your pre-conceived mold. Stop displaying your own goodness. Stop calling attention to your righteousness. Stop lusting to be noticed. Implied in this is the warning to beware of those who refuse to stop such behavior. And then, to blaze that warning into their memories, He went on to give three specific examples of how people show off their own righteousness so that others might ooh and aah over them.

Matthew 6:2 talks about "when you give alms" or when you are involved in acts of charity assisting others in need. He says don't "sound a trumpet" when you do this. Keep it quiet . . . even a secret (6:4). Don't scream for attention like Tarzan swinging through the jungle. Stay out of the picture, remain anonymous. Don't expect to have your name plastered all over the place. Pharisees *love* to show off their gifts to others. They *love* to be made over. They *love* to remind others who did this and that, or gave such and such to so and so. Jesus says: Don't show off when you use your money to help somebody out.

Matthew 6:5 talks about what to do "when you pray." He warns us against being supplicational showoffs who love to stand in prominent places and mouth meaningless mush in order to be seen and heard. Pharisees love syrupy words and sugar-crusted platitudes. They've got the technique for sounding high-and-holy down pat. Everything they say in their prayers causes listeners to think that this pious soul resides in heaven and was tutored at the feet of Michael the archangel and King James V. You're confident that they haven't had a dirty thought in the past 18 years . . . but you're also quietly aware that there's a huge chasm between what is coming out of the showoff's mouth and where your head is right then. Jesus says, Don't show off when you talk with the Father.

Matthew 6:16 talks about what to do "when you fast." Now that's the time the showoff really hits his stride. He works overtime trying to appear humble and sad, hoping to look hungry and exhausted like some freak who just finished crossing the Sahara that afternoon. "Do not be as the hypocrites!" Christ commands. Instead, we ought to look and sound fresh, clean and completely natural. Why? Because that's *real*—that's *genuine*—that's what He promises He will *reward*. Jesus says: Don't show off when you miss a couple or three meals.

Let's face it. Jesus spoke with jabbing, harsh words concerning the Pharisee. When it came to narrow legalism or self-righteous showing off, our Lord pulled no punches. He found it to be the only way to deal with those people who hung around the place of worship disdaining and despising other people. No less than seven times He pronounced "Woe to you"—because that's the only language a Pharisee understands, unfortunately.

Two final comments:

First . . . if you tend toward Pharisaism in any form, *stop it!* If you are the type of person who tries to bully others and look down at others (all the while thinking how impressed God must be to have you on His team) you are a 20th-century Pharisee. And frankly, that includes some who wear longer hair and prefer a guitar to a pipe organ. Pharisees can also delight in looking "cool."

Second . . . if a modern-day Pharisee tries to control your life, *stop him! Stop her!* Remind the religious phony that the splinter within your eye is between you and your Lord, and to pay attention to the tree trunk in his own eye. Chances are, however, that once an individual is infected, he will go right on nit-picking and self-praising for the rest of his shallow life, choked by the thorns of his own conceit. Pharisees, remember, are terribly hard of listening.